Maths Out Loud

Year 4

by
Sheila Ebbutt and Fran Mosley

Acknowledgements

Jane Prothero and Woodlands Primary School, Leeds

Karen Holman and Paddox Primary School, Rugby

Heather Nixon and Gayhurst Primary School, Buckinghamshire

John Ellard and Kingsley Primary School, Northampton

Jackie Smith, Catherine Torr and Roberttown CE J & I School, Kirklees

Wendy Price and St Martin's CE Primary School, Wolverhampton

Helen Elis Jones, University of Wales, Bangor

Ruth Trundley, Devon Curriculum Services, Exeter

Trudy Lines and Bibury CE Primary School, Gloucestershire

Elaine Folen and St Paul's Infant School, Surrey

Jane Airey and Frith Manor Primary School, Barnet

Beverley Godfrey, South Wales Home Educators' Network

Kay Brunsdon and Gwyrosydd Infant School, Swansea

Keith Cadman, Wolverhampton Advisory Services

Helen Andrews and Blue Coat School, Birmingham

Oakridge Parochial School, Gloucestershire

The Islington BEAM Development Group

Published by BEAM Education
Nelson Thornes
Delta Place, 27 Bath Road
Cheltenham, Gloucestershire, GL53 7TH
Tel 01242 278287
Fax 01242 253695
Email cservices@nelsonthrones.com
www.beam.co.uk
© Beam Education 2006, a division of Nelson Thornes
All rights reserved. None of the material in this
book may be reproduced in any form without prior
permission of the publisher
11 12 / 4 5
ISBN 978 1 903142 86 5
British Library Cataloguing-in-Publication Data
Data available
Edited by Ros Elphinstone and Marion Dill
Designed by Malena Wilson-Max
Photographs by Len Cross
Thanks to Rotherfield Primary School
Printed and bound Great Britain by Berforts Group
Reprinted in 2011

Contents

Introduction

Language plays an important part in the learning of mathematics – especially oral language. Children's relationship to the subject, their grasp of it and sense of ownership all depend on discussion and interaction – as do the social relationships that provide the context for learning. A classroom where children talk about mathematics is one that will help build their confidence and transform their whole attitude to learning.

Why is speaking and listening important in maths?
- Talking is creative. In expressing thoughts and discussing ideas, children actually shape these ideas, make connections and hone their definitions of what words mean.
- You cannot teach what a word means – you can only introduce it, explain it, then let children try it out, misuse it, see when it works and how it fits with what they already know and, eventually, make it their own.
- Speaking and listening to other children involves and motivates children – they are more likely to learn and remember than when engaging silently with a textbook or worksheet.
- As you listen to children, you identify children's misconceptions and realise which connections (between bits of maths) they have not yet made.

How does this book help me include 'speaking and listening' in maths?
- The lessons are structured to use and develop oral language skills in mathematics. Each lesson uses one or more classroom techniques that foster the use of spoken language and listening skills.
- The grid on p17 shows those speaking and listening objectives that are suitable for developing through the medium of mathematics. Each lesson addresses one of these objectives.
- The lessons draw on a bank of classroom techniques which are described on p8. These techniques are designed to promote children's use of speaking and listening in a variety of ways.

How does 'using and applying mathematics' fit in with these lessons?
- Many of the mathematical activities in this book involve problem solving, communication and reasoning, all key areas of 'using and applying mathematics' (U&A). Where this aspect of a lesson is particularly significant, this is acknowledged and expanded on in one of the 'asides' to the main lesson.

What about children with particular needs?
- For children who have impaired hearing, communication is particularly important, as it is all too easy for them to become isolated from their peers. Speaking and listening activities, even if adapted, simplified or supported by an assistant, help such children be a part of their learning community and to participate in the curriculum on offer.

- Children who speak English as an additional language benefit from speaking and listening activities, especially where these are accompanied by diagrams, drawings or the manipulation of numbers or shapes, which help give meaning to the language. Check that they understand the key words needed for the topic being discussed and, where possible, model the activity, paying particular attention to the use of these key words. Remember to build in time for thinking and reflecting on oral work.
- Differences in children's backgrounds affect the way they speak to their peers and adults. The lessons in this book can help children acquire a rich repertoire of ways to interact and work with others. Children who are less confident with written forms can develop confidence through speaking and listening.
- Gender can be an issue in acquiring and using speaking and listening skills. Girls may be collaborative and tentative, while boys sometimes can be more assertive about expressing their ideas. Address such differences by planning different groups, partners, classroom seating and activities. These lessons build on children's strengths and challenge them in areas where they are less strong.

What are the 'personal skills' learning objectives?

- There is a range of personal and social skills that children need to develop across the curriculum and throughout their school career. These include enquiry skills, creative thinking skills and ways of working with others. Some are particularly relevant to the maths classroom, and these are listed on the grid on p18.

What about assessment?

- Each lesson concludes with a section called 'Assessment for learning', which offers suggestions for what to look out for during the lesson and questions to ask in order to assess children's learning of all three learning objectives. There is also help on what may lie behind children's failure to meet these objectives and suggestions for teaching that might rectify the situation.
- Each section of four lessons includes a sheet of self-assessment statements to be printed from the accompanying CD-ROM and to be filled in at the end of each lesson or when all four are completed. Display the sheet and also give children their own copies. Then go through the statements, discussing and interpreting them as necessary. Ask children to complete their self-assessments with a partner they frequently work with. They should each fill in their own sheet, then look at it with their partner who adds their own viewpoint.

How can I make the best use of these lessons?

- Aim to develop a supportive classroom climate, where all ideas are accepted and considered, even if they may seem strange or incorrect. You will need to model this yourself in order for children to see what acceptance and open-mindedness look like.
- Create an ethos of challenge, where children are required to think about puzzles and questions.
- Slow down. Don't expect answers straight away when you ask questions. Build in thinking time where you do not communicate with the children, so that they have to reflect on their answers before making them. Expect quality rather than quantity.
- Model the language of discussion. Children who may be used to maths being either 'correct' or 'incorrect' need to learn by example what debate means. Choose a debating partner from the class, or work with another adult, and demonstrate uncertainty, challenge, exploration, questioning ...
- Tell children what they will be learning in the lesson. Each lesson concludes with an 'Assessment for learning' section offering suggestions for what to look out for to assess children's learning of all three learning objectives. Share these with the children at the start of the lesson to involve them in their own learning process.

How should I get the best out of different groupings?

- Get children used to working in a range of different groupings: pairs, threes or fours or as a whole class.
- Organise pairs in different ways on different occasions: familiar maths partners (who can communicate well); pairs of friends (who enjoy working together); children of differing abilities (who can learn something from each other); someone they don't know (to get them used to talking and listening respectfully to any other person).
- Give children working in pairs and groups some time for independent thought and work.
- Support pairs when they prepare to report back to the class. Go over with them what they have done or discovered and what they might say about this. Help them make brief notes – just single words or phrases – to remind them what they are going to say. If you are busy, ask an assistant or another child to take over your role. Then, when it comes to feedback time, support them by gentle probes or questions: "What did you do next?" or "What do your notes say?"

Classroom techniques used in this book

Ways of working

Peer tutoring

pairs of children

good for

This technique can benefit both the child who is being 'taught' and also the 'tutor' who develops a clearer understanding of what they themselves have learned and, in explaining it, can make new connections and solidify old ones. Children often make the best teachers, because they are close to the state of not knowing and can remember what helped them bridge the gap towards understanding.

how to organise it

'Peer tutoring' can work informally – children work in mixed ability pairs, and if one child understands an aspect of the work that the other doesn't, they work together in a tutor/pupil relationship to make sure the understanding is shared by both. Alternatively, you can structure it more formally. Observe children at work and identify those who are confident and accurate with the current piece of mathematics. Give them the title of 'Expert' and ask them to work with individuals needing support. Don't overuse this: the tutor has a right to work and learn at their own level, and tutoring others should only play a small part in their school lives.

Talking partners

pairs of children

good for

This technique helps children develop and practise the skills of collaboration in an unstructured way. Children can articulate their thinking, listen to one another and support each other's learning in a 'safe' situation.

how to organise it

Pairs who have previously worked together (for example, 'One between two', below) work together informally. The children in these pairs have had time to build up trust between them, and should have the confidence to tackle a new, less structured task. If you regularly use 'Talking partners', pairs of children will get used to working together. This helps them develop confidence, but runs the risk that children mutually reinforce their misunderstandings. In this case, changing partners occasionally can bring fresh life to the class by creating new meetings of minds.

One between two

pairs of children

good for

This technique helps children develop their skills of explaining, questioning and listening – behaviours that are linked to positive learning outcomes. Use it when the children have two or more problems or calculations to solve.

how to organise it

Pairs share a pencil (or calculator or other tool), and each assumes one of two roles: 'Solver' or 'Recorder'. (Supplying just one pencil encourages children to stay in role by preventing the Solver from making their own notes.)

The Solver has a problem and works through it out loud. The Recorder keeps a written record of what the Solver is doing. If the Solver needs something written down or a calculation done on the calculator, they must ask the Recorder to do this for them. If the Recorder is not sure of what the Solver is doing, they ask for further explanations, but do not engage in actually solving the problem. After each problem, children swap roles.

Introduce this way of working by modelling it yourself with a confident child partner: you talk through your own method of solving a problem, and the child records this thought process on the board.

Barrier games
pairs of children

good for

This technique helps children focus on spoken language rather than gesture or facial expression. The children must listen carefully to what is said, because they cannot see the person speaking.

how to organise it

Barrier games focus on giving and receiving instructions. Pairs of children work with a book or screen between them, so that they cannot see each other's work. The speaker gives information or instructions to the listener. The listener, in turn, asks questions to clarify understanding and gain information.

Eyes closed, eyes open
any number of children

good for

Depending on how this technique is used, it can either encourage children to listen carefully, because they cannot rely on visual checks, or to look carefully, because something was changed while they were not looking and they now need to identify this change.

how to organise it

Do this with the class: ask them to close their eyes while you count (slipping in a deliberate error) or drop coins into a tin. They must listen carefully to identify what you have done. Children then can do a similar activity in pairs.

Or tell children to close their eyes while you make one change in a sequence of numbers, pattern of shapes or some other structured set. When children open their eyes, they must spot what you have done and describe it or instruct you how to undo the change. Again, pairs can then carry on doing this independently.

Rotating roles
groups of various sizes

good for

Working in a small group to solve a problem encourages children to articulate their thinking and support each other's learning.

how to organise it

Careful structuring discourages individuals from taking the lead too often. Assign different roles to the children in the group: Chairperson, Reader, Recorder, Questioner, and so on. Over time, everyone has a turn at each role. You may wish to give children 'role labels' to remind them of their current role.

When you introduce this technique, model the role of chairperson in a group, with the rest of the class watching. Show how to include everyone and then discuss with the children what you have done, so as to make explicit techniques that they can use.

Discussion

Think, pair, share
groups of four

good for

Putting pairs together to work as a group of four helps avoid the situation where children in pairs mutually reinforce their common misunderstandings. It gives children time to think on their own, rehearse their thoughts with a partner and then discuss in a larger group. This encourages everyone to join in and discourages the 'quick thinkers' from dominating a discussion.

how to organise it

The technique is a development of 'Tell your partner' and involves the following:
* One or two minutes for individuals to think about a problem or statement and, possibly, to jot down their initial thoughts
* Two or three minutes where individuals work in pairs to share their thoughts
* Four or five minutes for two pairs to join together and discuss
* If you wish, you can also allow ten minutes for reporting back from some or all groups and whole-class discussion.

You can vary this pattern and the timings, but always aim to give children some 'private' thinking time.

Talking stick
any number of children

good for

Giving all children a turn at speaking and being listened to.

how to organise it

Provide the class with decorated sticks, which confer status on whoever holds them. Then, in a small or large group (or even the whole class), make it the rule that only the person holding the stick may speak, while the other children listen. You can use the stick in various ways: pass it around the circle; tell the child with the stick to pass it to whoever they want to speak next; have a chairperson who decides who will hold the stick next; ask the person with the stick to repeat what the previous person said before adding their own comments or ideas.

Tell your partner

pairs

good for

Whole-class question-and-answer sessions favour the quick and the confident and do not provide time and space for slower thinkers. This technique involves all children in answering questions and in discussion.

how to organise it

Do this in one of two ways:
- When you have just asked a question or presented an idea to think about, ask each child to turn to their neighbour or partner and tell them the answer. They then take turns to speak and to listen.
- Work less formally, simply asking children to talk over their ideas with a partner. Children may find this sharing difficult at first. They may not value talking to another child, preferring to talk to the teacher or not expressing their ideas at all. In this case, do some work on listening skills such as timing 'a minute each way' or repeating back to their partner what they have just said.

Devil's advocate

any number of children

good for

Statements – false or ambiguous as well as true – are often better than questions at provoking discussion.

how to organise it

In discussion with children, take the role of 'Devil's advocate', in which you make statements for them to agree or disagree with and to argue about.
To avoid confusing children by making false statements yourself, mention 'a friend' or 'someone you know' who makes these statements (a version of the 'silly teddy' who, in Nursery and Reception, makes mistakes for the children to correct). Alternatively, explain that when you make statements with your hands behind your back, your fingers may be crossed and you may be saying things that are not true.

Reporting back

Ticket to explain
Individuals

good for

This is a way of structuring feedback which helps children get the maximum out of offering explanations to the class. Everyone hears a method explained twice, and children have to listen carefully to their peers, rather than simply think about their own method.

how to organise it

When individuals want to explain their method of working to the class, their 'ticket' to be able to do this is to re-explain the method demonstrated by the child immediately before them. Or children work with a partner and explain their ideas to each other. When called on to speak, they explain their partner's idea and then their own.

Heads or tails
pairs of children

good for

When pairs of children work together, one child may rely heavily on the other to make decisions and to communicate or one child may take over, despite the efforts of the other child to have a say. This technique encourages pairs to work together to understand something and helps prevent an uneven workload.

how to organise it

Invite pairs to the front of the class to explain their ideas or solutions. When they get to the front, ask them to nominate who is heads and who is tails, then toss a coin to decide which of them does the talking. They have one opportunity to 'ask a friend' (probably their partner). As all children in the class know that they may be chosen to speak in this way, because the toss of the coin could make either of them into the 'explainer', they are motivated to work with their partner to reach a common understanding. Assigning the choice of explainer to the toss of a coin stops children feeling that anyone is picking on them personally (do warn them in advance, though!). Variation: If a pair of children has different ideas on a topic, ask both to offer explanations of each other's ideas.

1, 2, 3, 4
groups of four

good for

This technique offers the same benefits as 'Heads or tails', but is used for groups of four children rather than pairs.

how to organise it

This is a technique identical to 'Heads or tails', but with groups of four. Instead of tossing a coin, children are numbered 1 to 4, and the speaker is chosen by the roll of a dice (if 5 or 6 come up, simply roll again).

Additional techniques

Below are some further classroom techniques that are referred to in the lessons in this book.

Ideas board

whole class

good for

An ideas board is a place where children display their work to the rest of the class informally and quickly. It also provides a useful place for you to record ideas and problems that you want children to think about.

how to organise it

The visual aspect of display is not a priority with an ideas board – it is more like a notice board where ideas and information can be shared. Make sure you remove items regularly to keep it fresh and up to date.

Chewing the fat

any number of children

good for

Leaving ideas or questions unresolved provides thoughtful children with the opportunity to extend their thinking and can help develop good habits. Many real mathematicians like to have problems to think about in odd moments, just as some people like crossword clues or chess moves to occupy their mind.

how to organise it

Sometimes end a lesson with ideas, problems or challenges for children to ponder in their own time as you may have run out of time or one of the children has come up with a question or an idea which can only be discussed the next day.

Charts

Classroom techniques

This chart shows which of the classroom techniques previously described are used in which lessons.

	NUMBERS AND THE NUMBER SYSTEM	FRACTIONS, DECIMALS, PERCENTAGES, RATIO AND PROPORTION	ADDITION AND SUBTRACTION	MULTIPLICATION AND DIVISION	HANDLING DATA	MEASURES	SHAPE AND SPACE
	Lesson	Lesson	Lesson	Lesson	Lesson	Lesson	Lesson
One between two		7					28
Talking partners	3	6				22	
Rotating roles							26, 27
Peer tutoring				16		24	
Eyes closed, eyes open			10				
Barrier games	1					21	25
Talking stick		5			20		
Tell your partner	2		11	13			
Devil's advocate						23	
Think, pair, share	4			14, 15	18		
Ticket to explain		8	9				
Heads or tails / 1, 2, 3, 4			12		17, 19		

Speaking and listening skills

This chart shows which speaking and listening skills are practised in which lessons.

	NUMBERS AND THE NUMBER SYSTEM	FRACTIONS, DECIMALS, PERCENTAGES, RATIO AND PROPORTION	ADDITION AND SUBTRACTION	MULTIPLICATION AND DIVISION	HANDLING DATA	MEASURES	SHAPE AND SPACE
	Lesson	Lesson	Lesson	Lesson	Lesson	Lesson	Lesson
Explain and justify thinking	2	6	10, 11	13	17, 19		
Use precise language to explain ideas or give information		5				21, 24	
Share and discuss ideas and reach consensus	4		12	14			
Reach a common understanding with a partner	3			16			
Contribute to small-group and whole-class discussion				15	18, 20	22, 23	26, 27
Listen with sustained concentration	1	8	9				25
Listen and follow instructions accurately		7					28

Personal skills

This chart shows which personal skills are practised in which lessons.

	NUMBERS AND THE NUMBER SYSTEM	FRACTIONS, DECIMALS, PERCENTAGES, RATIO AND PROPORTION	ADDITION AND SUBTRACTION	MULTIPLICATION AND DIVISION	HANDLING DATA	MEASURES	SHAPE AND SPACE
	Lesson	Lesson	Lesson	Lesson	Lesson	Lesson	Lesson
Organise work							
Plan ways to solve a problem; Plan a sequence of work		6		16			
Plan and manage a group task	2						26
Use different approaches to tackle a problem				14			
Organise findings			12				
Work with others							
Discuss and agree ways of working			9				
Work cooperatively with others		5			20		28
Overcome difficulties and recover from mistakes	1						
Show awareness and understanding of others' needs		7		13, 15		24, 25	25
Give feedback sensitively	3				18		
Improve learning and performance							
Reflect on learning	4		11				
Critically evaluate own work						21	
Assess learning progress			10				27
Take pride in work		8			19		
Develop confidence in own judgements					17	23	

Lessons

Numbers and the number system

Learning objectives

	Lessons			
	1	2	3	4
Ⓜ Maths objectives				
read and write whole numbers	●			
order four-digit numbers		●		
multiply and divide positive integers by 10			●	
investigate properties of numbers				●
Ⓢ Speaking and listening skills				
listen with sustained concentration	●			
explain and justify thinking		●		
reach a common understanding with a partner			●	
share and discuss ideas and reach consensus				●
Ⓟ Personal skills				
work with others: overcome difficulties and recover from mistakes	●			
organise work: plan and manage a group task		●		
work with others: give feedback sensitively			●	
improve learning and performance: reflect on learning				●

About these lessons

Lesson 1: Reading large numbers

 Read and write whole numbers

Children need to practise reading and writing large numbers to develop speed and confidence when dealing with them. This open-ended activity, set as a challenge to sustain interest, gives them such practice.

 Listen with sustained concentration

Classroom technique: Barrier game

When children cannot see each other or each other's work, they must communicate orally. In this lesson, the particular focus is on listening as well as checking when in doubt as to what was said.

 Work with others: overcome difficulties and recover from mistakes

Depending on the spoken word can be difficult if there are no visual clues. If children make mistakes, help them see how they can work more carefully, checking with their partner at each stage.

Lesson 2: Ordering numbers

 Order four-digit numbers

As children gain information from answers to their questions, they must check each number to see whether it meets the criterion. This requires them to focus on how the position of a digit affects the value of a number.

 Explain and justify thinking

Classroom technique: Tell your partner

In the introduction and plenary, the 'Tell your partner' technique is used to encourage children to discuss the information gained by asking questions and to explain why they think one question is more useful than another.

 Organise work: plan and manage a group task

The group activity is structured to support children in managing their task. However, they must take responsibility for following, and making good use of, this structure and for working as a team.

Lesson 3: Multiplying and dividing by 10

 Multiply and divide positive integers by 10

Once children understand a general rule in mathematics, they have access to knowledge without the need to memorise much at all. In this lesson, children establish rules for multiplication and division by 10 and discuss any possible misconceptions.

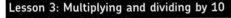 **Reach a common understanding with a partner**

Classroom technique: Talking partners

In this activity, children practise the skills of discussion and collaboration in an unstructured way. Try to pair up children who have previously worked together and had time to build up mutual trust. This will give them more confidence to tackle this fairly open-ended task.

 Work with others: give feedback sensitively

In the plenary, children turn to their partner and say one thing they have enjoyed about working together on the task. This type of affirmation helps build a class ethos of mutual respect and appreciation.

Lesson 4: Properties of numbers

 Investigate properties of numbers

Investigating number properties helps develop a creative and playful attitude to mathematics, allowing children to enhance their own understanding of the world of numbers.

 Share and discuss ideas and reach consensus

Classroom technique: Think, pair, share

This is a development of the 'Tell your partner' technique and involves children thinking about a problem alone before sharing their thoughts in pairs, then discussing in a group of four. It is an excellent way of encouraging children to share and discuss ideas and reach consensus.

 Improve learning and performance: reflect on learning

Encouraging children to reflect on what they have learned in a lesson helps them take responsibility for their own learning and gives them an opportunity to think about themselves objectively.

Reading large numbers
Classroom technique: Barrier game

Learning objectives

m **Maths**
Read and write
whole numbers

Speaking and listening
'Listen well'
Listen with sustained
concentration

Personal skills
'Get over difficulties
and mistakes'
Work with others: overcome
difficulties and recover
from mistakes

W **Words and phrases**
digit, thousands,
hundreds, tens, ones,
position, check

r **Resources**
display copy of RS2
for each pair:
wipe board
copy of RS1 (each cut
in half lengthwise)

Introduction

Display a place value grid to the class. Use counters to show three or four digits.

Th	H	T	O
••		•••	•

Children work in pairs and write these numbers on a shared wipe board.

m *How is the value of this 3 different from the value of this 3?*

3413

☺ *Why is it incorrect to call this number 242?*

Th	H	T	O
••		••• ••	••

Pairs

Children work back to back with their partners, with half of RS1 each. Child A draws eight spots anywhere on the first row of their grid to represent a number. They read out that number to their partner. Child B writes this in the first row of their grid, using digits.

Thousands	Hundreds	Tens	Ones
••	•••	•• •	•

Thousands	Hundreds	Tens	Ones
2	3	2	1

Pairs continue (always using eight spots) until each child has five numbers. They then compare sheets and check their work. They swap roles and repeat the exercise, aiming to make ten different numbers in all.

m *Supposing you put a zero here instead?*

m *What is the highest value number you can make with eight spots?*

☺ *Repeat the number that Harry just read out.*

☺ *How can you read out the number so that Nitya understands you?*

What have you learned from these mistakes?

Support: Children make three-digit numbers. They work together and read out the numbers to each other.

Extend: Children work with five-digit numbers.

Plenary

Help pairs make a critical evaluation of what they have learned.

Display one question from RS2 and read it out. Give children half a minute to think about how to answer that question and a minute to discuss this with their partner.

Take a few examples from the class and note any common experiences. Repeat this process for the other questions.

m *Most of you said, "Be careful with a zero."*

Drew says it helps to listen if you look at someone. Are there any other ideas?

Asha said they realise that they need to check their work.

Overcoming difficulties
Emphasise that you want children to listen carefully and to check with their partner if they are unsure about what was said or don't understand anything.

Assessment for learning

Can the children

m Read out and write four- or five-digit whole numbers?

Repeat the number their partner has just said?

Identify mistakes and think about how to learn from them?

If not

m Do more work using place value grids and counters.

Read out one part of the number at a time for the child to repeat: "Three thousand... two hundred... and twelve."

Hold a class discussion about errors and collect strategies for dealing with them.

Ordering numbers
Classroom technique: Tell your partner

Learning objectives

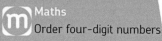 **Maths**
Order four-digit numbers

Speaking and listening
'Explain what you think and why you think it'
Explain and justify thinking

Personal skills
'Manage a group task'
Organise work: plan and manage a group task

Words and phrases
digit, thousands, hundreds, tens, ones, position, greater than, less than, information, check

Resources
display copy of RS3
for each group:
cards cut out from RS3
or RS4
wipe boards

Tell your partner
The blanks on RS3 are for the children to fill in as they please. Ask them to discuss with their neighbour how to use these open questions to extract useful information: "Is it between 3000 and 5000?"

A simpler option
Give each group an uncut copy of RS3, for children to choose which questions to ask.

Mini-plenary
Stop the class at some point in the session. Discuss which questions are useful in seeking to identify a mystery number and collect strategies for filling in the blanks on RS3.

Managing a group task
Ask groups to share the work and make sure each member has opportunities to decide, to act and to learn.

Introduction

Ask the class for eight four-digit numbers and write these up on the board.

Secretly, choose one of the eight numbers as your mystery number and make a note of it. The class must ask questions to identify this number.

Display the first question on RS3.

Give the answer to the question and help the class use the information to eliminate numbers from those displayed.

4592	3408
1526	2731
~~7038~~	1499
2307	~~6612~~

Continue like this with the other questions until the children have identified your number.

How do you know a number is more than 5000?

Discuss with your neighbour whether both those two numbers are greater than 3500.

Groups of three

Children work in groups of three. Each child in the group writes three four-digit numbers on a shared wipe board to make nine numbers in all. Give each group a set of question cards cut from RS3, which the children spread out on the table, face up.

One child chooses a number in secret and writes it down. The other two discuss which question to ask. The aim is to identify the chosen number by eliminating the others. They discard each question once they have asked it.

They continue until the number is identified.

Children take turns to be the person who chooses a number.

Tell us why you chose that number.

*Why is it not a good idea to ask a question naming a specific number –
for example, "Is it 4022?" Tell your neighbour what you think.*

How could you share the work more evenly?

Support: Work with three-digit numbers and questions from RS4.

Extend: Children invent more four-digit numbers. They devise their own questions
and find the mystery number with as few questions as possible.

Plenary

Present eight or ten four-digit numbers and, again, choose one in secret. Tell
children to think up and ask their own questions to identify your chosen number,
using as few questions as possible.

The hundreds digit is greater than 5. So which numbers can't it be?

Could you get my number with just one question? How?

Tell your partner

Children discuss and agree with
a neighbour a useful question.
Ask two or three pairs for their
question and ask them to explain
why they think it is useful.

Assessment for learning

Can the children

Recognise all the numbers that are greater than
a given number?

Explain why they filled the blank in a question
the way they did?

Organise themselves to fulfil the task successfully?

If not

Use a base board to display a number, then
rearrange the same digits to make a different
number. Discuss the changes made and how they
affect the value of each digit.

Do more activities with the class that involve
elimination by 'Yes' or 'No' questioning. Discuss
which questions would be useful, and why.

Help a group that has been successful at
managing the task talk to the class about what
they did, and did not, do to achieve this success.

Multiplying and dividing by 10
Classroom technique: Talking partners

Introduction

Present these numbers on the board.

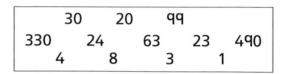

Use a display calculator to multiply or divide each number in turn by 10. Ask the class to predict each answer as you go along. Don't yet formulate any rules about dividing or multiplying by 10.

Tell children that you want them to concentrate on working well with their partner, because, in the plenary, they are going to give feedback on how well the partnership worked.

(m) *Tell your partner what you think the answer will be, and why you think that.*

Wipe board
Children decide in pairs the answer they expect and write this on wipe boards to hold up.

Pairs

Children choose a mixture of one-, two- and three-digit numbers and multiply and divide those numbers by 10. They record the results systematically. They can check their work with a calculator if they wish.

They then work together to write down their own rules for how multiplying and dividing by 10 works.

(m) *Look at the calculator display. What happens to the 3 when you multiply it by 10? And by 100?*

(m) *How could you check that rule? Does it work for any number?*

(🗣) *Geoff, read through your rule. Hari, are you satisfied that it makes sense?*

How are you two sharing the work? What is your partner doing there? And what is your role?

U&A General statements
We want children to be able to generalise for themselves the rules behind mathematical operations.

Questioning
Pairs swap work and check each other's statements to see if they agree with them.

Support: Provide a place value board and number cards to model the numbers.

Extend: Ask for rules for multiplying or dividing by 100 or 1000.

Addressing misconceptions

Look out for explanations that suggest an incomplete understanding of the process, such as: "23 divided by 10 is 2.3, so when you divide by 10, you put in a decimal point." Encourage pairs to discuss the validity of such ideas. Model the operation on a place value board to show that what always happens is that the digits moves and a decimal point is inserted if necessary – for example, when dividing 30 by 10, a decimal point is not needed.

Giving feedback

If children are unfamiliar with giving this sort of feedback, you could model it in a role-play scenario with a child.

Plenary

A few pairs present one of their written explanations. The rest of the class agree rules for each operation and write these up.

> **Multiplying by 10**
> Move all the numbers one place to the left. Then put a 0 in the extra space.
>
> **Dividing by 10**
> Move all the numbers one place to the right.

Pairs then turn to their partner and tell them one thing they have enjoyed about working together today.

(m) *Do we really 'add a nought'? What is the zero for?*

(m) *Does it matter what size of number you start with?*

(⇄) *Talk to your partner about the idea that when you divide by 10, you just cross out the last digit. Is that ever true? Always true?*

(☺) *Think about an aspect of working with your partner that you enjoyed.*

Assessment for learning

Can the children

(m) Multiply and divide these numbers by 10: 40, 9, 95, 125, 104?

(⇄) Explain to you what their partner has just said?

(☺) Find appropriate things to say when asked to give feedback?

If not

(m) heck whether the problem is with accuracy, with reading numbers or with the child's understanding of place value and decimals. Help children model numbers with the aid of a place value board.

(⇄) Ask the child's partner to say their piece in short chunks, then ask the child to repeat these chunks to you. Make sure children are working with partners with whom they feel comfortable.

(☺) Ask children to reflect on their own skills at working together, out loud or on paper, and ask their partners whether or not they agree with what has been said.

Properties of numbers
Classroom technique: Think, pair, share

Learning objectives

m **Maths**
Investigate properties of numbers

Speaking and listening
'Share ideas and reach agreement'
Share and discuss ideas and reach consensus

Personal skills
'Think about what you have learned'
Improve learning and performance: reflect on learning

W **Words and phrases**
number property, even, odd, multiple, investigate, explore, rule, pattern, prime

r **Resources**
counters
cubes
squared paper
calculators
number lines

Tell your neighbour
Children turn to their neighbour and discuss one way in which the two numbers are different.

Think, pair, share
Individuals think about the problem in silence, then share it with a partner. They record as many ideas as they can think of. After a few minutes, pairs combine into groups of four and pool their ideas. Groups prepare both a spoken and a written presentation of their results for the class.

Preparing for the plenary
Remind children that they may be asked to represent their group in the plenary, so all four members of the group should be prepared to speak. Identify one or two groups with interesting or well-presented results to call on in the plenary.

Introduction

Write up two numbers and the question 'How are these numbers different?' Ask children to discuss briefly in pairs some ways in which the two numbers are different.

Then take suggestions and scribe these.

Use equipment to model children's ideas or to check facts.

How are these numbers different?	
20	**21**
multiple of 4	not a multiple of 4
two ten-sticks of cubes	odd
even	Say it when you
5 of it make 100	count in threes.
Say it when you count	21 is closer to 100.
in fives.	

m *Show me on the number line how you know that five 20s make 100.*

Talk with your neighbour about whether there are any other facts to add to the list.

Groups of four

Present the class with another pair of numbers such as 13 and 15. Use 'Think, pair, share' (p10) to get children to explore and record how these two numbers are different.

Children use any equipment available in the classroom if they need to.

m *If it's a multiple of 2, what else do you know about it?*

Talk together about how to use counters or cubes or a calculator to help you.

Have you learned any new ideas from the group? Can you say what they are?

Support: Make sure that children have apparatus available. Work with groups that need extra support.

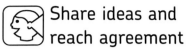

Share ideas and reach agreement

Extend: Suggest that children find ways in which the numbers are the same and ways in which they are different. Introduce the word 'prime' to describe numbers that cannot be broken up into equal groups.

Plenary

One or two of the groups present their ideas orally.

Children in the other groups listen and tick off on their lists any ideas that are the same. Children can suggest ways to refine the statements offered. Record agreed wording on the board.

Invite the other groups, in turn, to present any ideas that have not yet been mentioned and add these to the list. Include groups who tackled similarities as well as differences.

1, 2, 3, 4
Use this technique (see p12) to choose which member of a group will speak.

Ideas board
Introduce an 'Ideas board' (p13). Leave up the list for children to look at in the next few days and add ideas of their own.

13 and 15 – differences	13 and 15 – similarities
13 counters don't make a rectangle, but 15 do.	1 in the tens place
13 is prime, and 15 is not.	less than 20
15 is half of a tens number, but 13 isn't.	teens number
	odd
	made up of odd digits

Children reflect silently for a minute, then turn to their partner and tell them one thing they have learned today.

(m) *How do you know that 13 is odd?*

(📖) *What do you think this group mean when they say 15 makes a rectangle? Talk about it with your group.*

Think about whether any of the ideas in the lesson were new to you.

Assessment for learning

Can the children

(m) Use a range of ideas to distinguish the properties of two numbers?

(📖) Say whether or not they agree with another child's statement, and why?

(🙂) Identify one or more ideas from the lesson that they haven't thought of before?

If not

(m) Consider introducing new ideas by suggesting that the child shares ideas with another group.

(📖) Help children express their ideas in a different way if they lack mathematical understanding or language skills.

(🙂) Go through the list of differences with the child and ask which of the ideas are new. Consider whether the child may be working at a level below their ability.

Name _____

Self and peer assessment

Lesson 1: Reading large numbers	I think	My partner thinks
(m) I can read out these numbers: 213, 1025, 1904, 19 807		
I can repeat the number my partner has just read out.		
If I did this work again, I would know how to avoid making mistakes.		

Lesson 2: Ordering numbers	I think	My partner thinks
(m) I can say which of three numbers is the largest/smallest.		
I can explain whether a question is useful in identifying a mystery number.		
I am good at taking turns.		

Name _____

Lesson 3: Multiplying and dividing by 10	I think	My partner thinks
(m) I know how to multiply and divide any number by 10.		
(⊗) I talk with my partner about our work.		
(☺) I give feedback sensitively to my partner.		

Lesson 4: Properties of numbers	I think	My partner thinks
(m) I can describe how two numbers are different.		
(⊗) I can explain my ideas so that my partner understands me.		
(☺) I know which ideas in this lesson are new to me.		

Self and peer assessment

Fractions, decimals, percentages, ratio and proportion

Learning objectives

	Lessons			
	5	**6**	**7**	**8**
ⓜ Maths objectives				
find fractions of whole numbers	●			
recognise the equivalence of simple fractions		●		
compare and order familiar fractions			●	
use decimal notation and know what each digit represents				●
Ⓢ Speaking and listening skills				
use precise language to give information	●			
explain and justify thinking		●		
listen and follow instructions accurately			●	
listen with sustained concentration				●
Ⓟ Personal skills				
work with others: work cooperatively with others	●			
organise work: plan ways to solve a problem		●		
work with others: show awareness and understanding of others' needs			●	
improve learning and performance: take pride in work				●

About these lessons

Lesson 5: Fractions of a set

 Find fractions of whole numbers

In this activity, children use counters to design a string of tree lights with the rule that half the lights must be the same colour. This underlines the point that halves can be different sizes, depending on the wholes they are part of. It also gives children practice in using fractional language to describe their strings of lights.

 Use precise language to give information

Classroom technique: Talking stick

The child speaking holds the 'talking stick', which signals to the rest of the group that they are to be quiet and listen to that child. The child who is speaking describes their strings of lights to their group, using the precise language of fractions.

 Work with others: work cooperatively with others

Children share a finite resource – counters – and are encouraged to pay attention to how to share these in a friendly way. In addition, they check each other's work and, in the process, may need to consider how to point out errors tactfully.

Lesson 6: Fractions of a shape

 Recognise the equivalence of simple fractions

Working with shapes offers children a different model for fractions from the number model – and one that is complementary. Making connections between the different models gives children more opportunities of making sense of the mathematics of fractions.

 Explain and justify thinking

Classroom technique: Talking partners

Children work together on a task, aiming to work out the fraction represented by each piece and to explain how they know this. In the plenary, they may be called on to offer this explanation to the whole class.

 Organise work: plan ways to solve a problem

It may not be possible to know exactly how you will solve a problem in advance, but it is useful to think about how to get started, to consider what tools or equipment might be useful and to plan how you will keep track of what you have done. Problems such as this provide opportunities for discussing these issues with children.

Lesson 7: Counting in quarters

 Compare and order familiar fractions

The number line gives children a sense of the pattern of numbers when counting with fractional numbers. In this activity, children complete number lines with intervals of a quarter. They then listen as you read out a part sequence and try to spot the deliberate mistake.

 Listen and follow instructions accurately

Classroom technique: One between two

One child has the pencil, and their partner tells them which fractions to write down. The child with the pencil must listen carefully, as they are only allowed to write what they are instructed to. However, they have the right to question whether what they have been told to do is correct.

 **Work with others: show awareness and understanding of others' needs**

Sharing a pencil and a task requires children to be sensitive to each other's needs: they must think about how to give instructions that their partner will understand, how to pace these instructions and how to deal sensitively with any mistakes their partner makes.

Lesson 8: Decimal notation

 Use decimal notation and know what each digit represents

Children need to think carefully about the value of each digit in a number to change one of the digits to a zero by subtracting a single number. Checking on a calculator reinforces the experience while also giving children a sense of control.

 Listen with sustained concentration

Classroom technique: Ticket to explain

In the plenary, children must listen carefully to what the others say, as they may be called on to speak next and, before doing so, must repeat the previous child's explanation.

 Improve learning and performance: take pride in work

Setting their own challenges allows children to work at a level where they can succeed and feel proud at having worked hard to achieve this success.

Fractions of a set
Classroom technique: Talking stick

Introduction

Introduce the idea of a string of tree lights, using coloured counters (or circles) on the overhead projector or whiteboard. Make a string of ten lights in two different colours.

Children talk to their neighbours about what fraction of the whole each colour represents.

Repeat this with a string of twelve lights in three different colours.

(m) *What does it mean when I say one light is a tenth of the whole string?*

(m) *Is one light still one tenth when we are working with twelve lights?*

Tell your partner
For example: "The string is $\frac{5}{10}$ red lights, $\frac{2}{10}$ green lights and $\frac{3}{10}$ yellow lights." Encourage simplifications such as '$\frac{1}{2}$ red' rather than '$\frac{5}{10}$ red', but don't insist on them.

Groups of four

Give each group of four a heap of coloured counters and each child a copy of RS5. The children use the counters to make strings of lights that fit the criteria described, record these on the sheet and then complete the statements for each string.

Working cooperatively
Tell children that sharing counters is an opportunity to practise working in a considerate and friendly way.

Checking
Remind children to check that each string matches the criteria listed. During the talking phase, ask the group to check that the description given by a child matches their drawing.

	of the lights are _____
	of the lights are _____
	of the lights are _____

When everyone in the group has completed their strings, give the group a 'talking stick'. Each child, in turn, shows their recording and describes their strings to the rest of their group, using the language of fractions.

Talking stick
Each child, in turn, holds the 'talking stick'. The rest of the group pay attention to the child with the stick.

(👤) *How can you describe your pattern of lights in a mathematical way?*

(😊) *Can you describe how you worked cooperatively with your group?*

Simplifying fractions
Encourage children to simplify their fractions.

Support: Use RS6 (a simplified version of RS5) and support children in making their fraction statements.

Extend: Use RS7 (a more complex version of RS5) and skip the stage of making the string of lights with counters. Suggest that children make up their own criteria for another child to fulfil.

Plenary

Ask children which colours they chose for their 'halves' and how many lights they had in that colour. Draw out the idea that halves can be different sizes, depending on the wholes of which they are part.

Equivalent fractions
Use counters on an overhead projector or circles on a whiteboard to form strings and rearrange the counters to demonstrate that, for example, [3] $\frac{9}{15}$ is the same as $\frac{3}{5}$.

Using 'Tell your partner' (p10), ask children to identify equivalents among the fractions they have been working with. Keep this short and simple.

(m) *Mayur made an 8-string and a 12-string, with half the lights in one colour. Are the two halves the same? How can 4 and 6 both be called 'half'?*

(m) *$\frac{4}{8}$ of these lights are red. What other fractions are worth the same as $\frac{4}{8}$?*

Tell your partner any fractions you found that are the same as one half.

Are there any other fractions you made that can be described in another way?

Assessment for learning

Can the children

(m) Explain why $\frac{5}{10}$ of a string of lights is the same as one half?

Use the appropriate fractions words ('one half', 'one twelfth', and so on) when describing their strings of lights?

Respect the rules about using the 'talking stick'?

If not

(m) Do some work on the meaning of 'a half' and 'a quarter', such as sorting objects into those that are, and are not, halved correctly, to reinforce the meaning of 'half'.

Do more work on fractions of a set with children. Revisit this idea regularly, using the children themselves as the 'set': "Two sixths of the children in this group have completed their work"; "One thirtieth of the class is away today."

Use the 'talking stick' in other class sessions. Emphasise why it is a valuable tool and be clear about the rules that must be observed in its use.

Fractions of a shape
Classroom technique: Talking partners

Learning objectives

(m) Maths
Recognise the equivalence of simple fractions

Speaking and listening
'Explain what you think and why you think it'
Explain and justify thinking

Personal skills
'Plan ways to solve a problem'
Organise work: plan ways to solve a problem

(W) Words and phrases
whole, fraction, halve, equal, half, quarter, eighth, sixteenth, explain, answer, justify, certain, check

(r) Resources
display copy of RS8
masking tape
wipe boards
for each pair:
copy of RS9
copy of RS8 (optional)
scissors

Involving all children
Children write the fraction on their wipe boards and hold these up for you to see.

Explaining and checking
Use a tangram cut into pieces and another whole tangram to demonstrate the relative sizes of the pieces, to back up the children's explanations:

"If this small square really is $\frac{1}{4}$ of the big square, it will fit on the big one four times."

Talking partners
Remind children that this is collaborative work: they must both participate in, and agree about, the decision making.

Planning work
Encourage children to talk together about how to tackle the problem: what they might do first, how this might help them with the next part, how to record their work, and so on.

Introduction

Display RS8 to the class and ask the children to identify the fractions of the whole represented by each shape.

(m) *How can we check that this square is worth a quarter of the whole?*

(Speaking) *Tell your partner what fraction of the whole each of these smaller triangles is. Say how you know that.*

Pairs

Give each pair a copy of RS9. Working together, children find out what fraction of the whole each of the pieces is, without cutting up the tangram.

Children keep notes on how they know what fraction of the whole each piece is.

(m) *What fraction is one triangle of the whole?*

(m) *What is half of a half? And half of a quarter?*

(Speaking) *How do you know these shapes are worth one eighth?*

(Personal) *What will you do first to help you start?*

Support: Children work with the simpler tangram on RS8. They cut up the tangram and compare pieces before progressing to RS9.

Extend: Children work out the fraction of the whole represented by any two pieces taken together.

Modelling

As in the introduction, refer to both a tangram that has been cut into pieces and a whole tangram square to demonstrate the relative sizes of the pieces. Children use these to back up their explanations.

Making connections

This activity links the shapes model of fractions with the number line model.

An optional follow-up

Use the tangram to make pictures. Then look together at some completed work and discuss the idea that they all used the same amount of paper. Challenge children to spot some fractions in the tangrams.

Plenary

Pairs explain their solutions and their methods of working these out, using the 'Heads or tails' technique (p12).

Draw a number line on the board, with the numbers 0 and 1 at either end and **!s** in the middle. Establish where **!f** and **!k** belong. The children work with you to position the pieces of the main tangram (RS10) along the number line in order of size. Stick the pieces on with masking tape. Keep some whole tangrams to hand to show whole and halve the whole as two triangles.

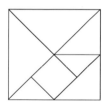

🗨 *Which pieces are smaller than $\frac{1}{2}$? How can you be sure?*

🗨 *If $\frac{1}{2}$ goes here, where does $\frac{1}{4}$ go? How do you know?*

🙂 *What did you do to find the fractions without cutting out the shapes?*

Assessment for learning

Can the children

Ⓜ Find a way to work out any of the fractions of the tangram?

🗨 Explain how they know what fraction of the whole square a piece is?

🙂 Suggest some things they might do to help them tackle the problem?

If not

Ⓜ Do more work with the children on the idea that the denominator of a fraction tells you how many of it are needed to make up the whole.

🗨 Invite a confident child to explain to the class how they know the size of one piece of the tangram. Then ask pairs to use this as a model for explaining.

🙂 Focus on the value of discussing with a partner how you will start a problem and what you need to do to keep track of your progress.

Counting in quarters
Classroom technique: One between two

Learning objectives

(m) Maths
Compare and order familiar fractions

Speaking and listening
'Listen and follow instructions'
Listen and follow instructions accurately

Personal skills
'Think about what other people need'
Work with others: show awareness and understanding of others' needs

(W) Words and phrases
one whole, half, quarter, three quarters, mixed number, order, position

(r) Resources
for each pair:
copy of RS10
pencil
wipe board

Offering structure
Filling in the whole numbers first provides a structure.

Involving all children
Pairs agree the next number you need, write it on their wipe board and show it to you.

One pencil between two
Child A has the pencil and sheet. Child B instructs them what numbers to write and how to write them. Child B does not write anything unless told to by their partner. However, they may query an instruction: "I don't think the next number is *three and two quarters*."

Introduction

Draw a segment of a number line on the board, with about 16 markers but no numbers.

Mark in zero and explain that this is a number line on which each interval is worth one quarter.

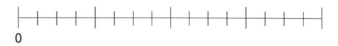

The children count with you along the line in quarters ("One quarter, two quarters, three quarters, four quarters, five quarters..."), pointing to the markers in turn. Then count along it again, saying the whole, half and quarter numbers ("One quarter, a half, three quarters, *one whole*, one and a quarter...").

Write the whole numbers in as you say them.

The children help you write in the proper fractions.

(m) *What comes next after 1? After 2? And after 3?*

(m) *What number do you expect on the marker before the whole number?*

(m) *What is the pattern in the numbers we are saying?*

Pairs

Each child completes one line from RS10, using the 'One between two' technique (p8), with one pencil between two.

Tell me the instruction your partner just gave you.

If your partner hasn't written what you wanted, what will you do?

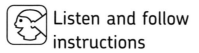
Thinking about others
Before they start their task, children think and talk about what behaviours they like and appreciate in someone they are working with.

Visualising
Eventually, children need to internalise an image of numbers in order. The aim is to help children develop an 'inner' number line.

Support: Children have a completed line to refer to.

Extend: Children write their own line on blank paper.

Plenary

Count with the class in quarters again, this time without a visual prop. Start at 0 or at other numbers.

Children listen as you count on (or back) from a number and make a deliberate mistake. Tell them to listen carefully, with their eyes closed, and put their hands up in silence when they spot the error.

(m) *Why doesn't the sequence go* 1, $1\frac{1}{4}$, $1\frac{1}{3}$?

(m) *What* does *come after 3?*

Assessment for learning

Can the children

(m) Spot when you make a deliberate error in the sequence of quarters?

(⟳) Stay silent and alert when their partner is telling them what to write?

(☺) Deal sensitively with any difficulties or mistakes on the part of their partner?

If not

(m) Practise counting in halves, thirds and quarters with the class, then introduce deliberate errors again and discuss why what you are saying is incorrect.

(⟳) Give children more practice in the 'One between two' technique (p8). Before using it again, talk to the class about why it is valuable and what they must do to make sure it works well.

(☺) Make sure to model this yourself and show how highly you value such sensitivity.

Decimal notation
Classroom technique: Ticket to explain

Tell your partner
Children confer with a neighbour about which keys they think you pressed.

Reporting back
Remind children at this stage that you may ask either of them to speak in the plenary – so both partners should be able to explain how they worked out each calculation.

Making up problems
This gives children the opportunity to think about their own level of understanding. Encourage them to work at a level that is sufficiently challenging.

Introduction

Use a calculator to display a decimal number to the class. In secret, subtract a number so that one of the digits changes to 0. Ask for ideas about what you did.

> $3.6 \rightarrow 3$ (subtract 0.6)
> $4.7 \rightarrow 0.7$ (subtract 4)

Explain what number you subtracted to get zero, and why.

m *Let's subtract 6, then 60, then 0.6, to see what happens.*

Pairs

Give each pair a copy of RS11 and a calculator. Pairs begin by working out mentally which number to subtract to change one number to another and record this. They then use the calculator to check their answer.

When pairs have completed the first half of the sheet, they invent their own decimal numbers for the second half. They complete and check as before.

m *What does that zero mean?*

@ *In the number 5.5, what is each 5 worth?*

@ *How could you make the next problem just a little bit harder for yourselves?*

Support: Children make the numbers using digit cards placed on the base board on RS12.

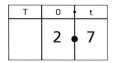 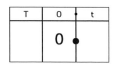

To get from 2.7 to 0.7, just remove the 2.
Check on the calculator: $2.7 - 2 = 0.7$

Extend: Children make up problems for another pair. They can try replacing more than one digit with zero: $38.7 \rightarrow 30$ or $24.7 \rightarrow 20$. Alternatively, they can change a digit to a number other than zero (involving addition or subtraction): $38.7 \rightarrow 48.7$ or $24.7 \rightarrow 24.9$.

Plenary

Pairs choose one printed problem from the sheet and one that they devised themselves and agree explanations of how to solve each of them.

Ask a child to explain one of their solutions. Model their explanation with the calculator display.

Repeat this with other children, using 'Ticket to explain' (p11).

As a class, discuss how to reverse the process, using a calculator.

> 30.7 → 36.7   (add 6)
>
> 403.3 → 443.3   (add 40)

Finally, pairs invent one last challenging problem and solve it.

Ⓜ *What is the best strategy for solving all these problems?*

🗪 *What do you have to do to repeat Chloë's explanation?*

☺ *What was the hardest problem you solved?*

Ticket to explain
Before children give their own explanation about a calculation, they must repeat what their partner said previously.

U&A General statements
Aim for a general explanation of how to solve any of these problems. Being able to see problems and solutions in general terms gives children a valuable overview of the mathematics involved.

Assessment for learning

Can the children

Ⓜ Replace the 3s with zeros in 3.4, 21.3, 439.2, 9313.2?

🗪 Accurately repeat the previous child's problem and solution?

☺ Identify a 'hard' problem that they feel pleased at being able to solve?

If not

Ⓜ Do more work on modelling decimal numbers on place value boards, using base-ten blocks, counters or digit cards.

🗪 Have a blitz on listening to each other and repeating what was said.

☺ Look with the child at their completed sheet and help them find a problem there that they feel they can congratulate themselves on being able to solve.

Self and peer assessment

Name _____

Lesson 5: Fractions of a set	I think	My partner thinks
(m) I can describe the fraction of each part of my pattern.		
I use fraction words such as one half and one twelfth to describe my pattern.		
I listen to others.		

Lesson 6: Fractions of a shape	I think	My partner thinks
(m) I can work out all of the fractions of the tangram.		
I can explain how I know what fraction of the whole tangram one piece is.		
I talk to my partner about how we can tackle the problem.		

Name _____

Lesson 7: Counting in quarters	I think	My partner thinks
(m) I can count in quarters up to:		
(face) I listen carefully when my partner is telling me what to write.		
(face) I think about how my partner needs me to behave.		

Lesson 8: Decimal notation	I think	My partner thinks
(m) I can replace any digit with zeros in this number:		
(face) I can repeat what someone else has just said.		
(face) I can invent a problem that is hard for me.		

Self and peer assessment

Addition and subtraction

Learning objectives

	Lessons			
	9	**10**	**11**	**12**
Ⓜ Maths objectives				
use known number facts and place value to add or subtract mentally	●			
know what to add to a two-digit number to make 100		●		
add several small numbers			●	
use addition to solve problems involving money				●
Ⓢ Speaking and listening skills				
listen with sustained concentration	●			
explain and justify thinking		●	●	
share and discuss ideas and reach consensus				●
Ⓟ Personal skills				
work with others: discuss and agree ways of working	●			
improve learning and performance: assess learning progress		●		
improve learning and performance: reflect on learning			●	
organise work: organise findings				●

About these lessons

Lesson 9: Using known number facts

 Use known number facts and place value to add or subtract mentally

Mental facility with numbers is partly about 'just knowing' and partly about making good use of what you know. In this activity, children think and talk about ways of building on a known addition or subtraction fact to derive a number of other facts.

 Listen with sustained concentration

Classroom technique: Ticket to explain

When a child is asked to explain their calculation to the class, their 'ticket' to do this is to re-explain what the child immediately before them said. This encourages children to listen carefully to their peers, rather than simply think about their own calculation.

 Work with others: discuss and agree ways of working

Collaborative working doesn't just happen. We need to help children develop the relevant skills. Spending time in this lesson on a class discussion about ways of working helps children think about how they work with a partner and provides an opportunity for change.

Lesson 10: Number pairs to 100

 Know what to add to a two-digit number to make 100

This is a number skill that has extra importance as we use it so often when working out, or checking, change from a pound. Children work on each number pair twice: first, they find what to add to a number to make it up to 100; then, one child changes a digit in secret for the other child to detect and correct.

 Explain and justify thinking

Classroom technique: Eyes closed, eyes open

This technique encourages children to look carefully and to think, because the numbers changed while they were not looking, and they need to identify this change. They must then explain how they know which numbers have been changed.

 Improve learning and performance: assess learning progress

Children are asked to make an informal judgement about whether they think they are getting more confident and accurate at this small but important piece of maths learning.

Lesson 11: Adding three small numbers

 Add several small numbers

Confidence and speed with manipulating small numbers is a prerequisite for success later on with more complex calculations. Games like this give children practice in, and an incentive for, repeatedly adding several numbers – which could easily be tedious in another context.

 Explain and justify thinking

Classroom technique: Tell your partner

Before children place a counter on the total they have chosen, they must explain clearly to their partner how they worked out the addition.

 Improve learning and performance: reflect on learning

Making and discussing a communal list of strategies for adding three numbers allows children to think about which of these they have learned to use and which they are not yet confident with.

Lesson 12: Solving money problems

 Use addition to solve problems involving money

Children can tackle this open-ended problem at different levels. But, at any level, they need to keep track of their decisions and calculations and think about ways of presenting the solution to the class.

 Share and discuss ideas and reach consensus

Classroom technique: 1, 2, 3, 4

Children are encouraged to share an understanding of the problem and its solution, because they 'own' it jointly (the problem is based on their own choices) and because they know that, in the plenary, any of the group may be called on to explain their working.

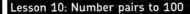 **Organise work: organise findings**

Organising written work is important as a way of keeping track of the process of problem solving and in order to make sense of the solution when presenting it to others. In this lesson, careful questioning can help children think about both aspects of organising their recording.

Using known number facts

Classroom technique: Ticket to explain

Learning objectives

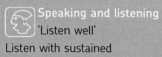

Maths
Use known number facts and place value to add or subtract mentally

Speaking and listening
'Listen well'
Listen with sustained concentration

Personal skills
'Discuss and agree how to work'
Work with others: discuss and agree ways of working

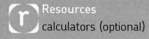

Words and phrases
digit, place, add, plus, total, altogether, double, subtract, take away, minus, is the same as, equals

Resources
calculators (optional)

Tell your partner/Ticket to explain

Ask each child to turn to their partner and tell them one new 'free fact'. Then ask a few children for their facts, together with explanations of how they derived them, using 'Ticket to explain' (p12). Keep this brief.

Level of difficulty

Starting with a simple addition draws in all children. Challenge more confident children with questions designed for them: "So what is 1.5 plus 1.5? And 15 × 8?"

Discuss and agree ways of working

Pairs consider together how best to share the work.

Introduction

Write up the calculation 15 + 15 = 30. Ask for 'free facts' that can be derived from that and write these up.

$$15 + 16 = 31 \qquad\qquad 150 + 150 = 300$$
$$15 + 25 = 40 - \mathbf{15 + 15 = 30} - 15 \times 2 = 30$$
$$30 - 15 = 15$$
$$300 - 150 = 150$$

(m) *Which calculations are like each other? Are there any more like that?*

(s) *Why do you disagree with that suggestion?*

(s) *What sort of calculation has nobody said yet?*

Pairs

Write up a new equation.

$$23 + 57 = 80$$

Pairs record this equation and its related 'free facts'.

(m) *How can you turn that addition fact into a subtraction fact?*

(m) *How do you know that 33 + 57 = 100 is wrong?*

(p) *How do you each know what to work on next?*

Support: Ask for explanations and encourage checking, especially with less confident children: "How do you work out that 80 – 23 is 57? How can you check it?"

Extend: Give children large numbers or decimals to work with.

Plenary

Collect a variety of the children's 'free facts' on the board.

Look out for any of the children's 'free facts' that can be used to emphasise a teaching point – for example, revise the fact that each addition fact gives you a 'partner' addition fact and two subtraction facts.

$$23 + 57 = 80 \rightarrow 57 + 23 = 80$$
$$80 - 23 = 57 \rightarrow 80 - 57 = 23$$

Look at other patterns children may have used.

(m) *Is there a limit to the facts that you could work out from this starter fact? Or could you go on forever? Why do you think that?*

(🗨) *What operation did Sam use for his new fact?*

(☺) *How do you come to an agreement if you first disagree?*

Ticket to explain
Keep up the pace by collecting the majority of 'free facts' without any explanation. Just occasionally, ask for an explanation and then ask the next child to repeat this explanation before they make their own contribution.

Assessment for learning

Can the children

(m) Derive a wide range of addition and subtraction facts from one original fact?

(🗨) Repeat the explanation given by another child?

(☺) Tell you how they have decided to share the work?

If not

(m) Work with some word problems that show an addition and its complementary subtraction – for example, a child combines 15p and 20p to make 35p, then loses 15p to leave 20p.

(🗨) Make a note to do more work on listening to simple explanations and repeating them to a partner.

(☺) Focus on the mechanics of sharing work for a while: deciding whether to have a pencil each or whether to share one; discussing where to start, rather than just diving in; offering suggestions; asking for explanations, and so on.

Number pairs to 100
Classroom technique: Eyes closed, eyes open

Learning objectives

(m) Maths
Know what to add to a two-digit number to make 100

(👥) Speaking and listening
'Explain what you think and why you think it'
Explain and justify thinking

(😊) Personal skills
'Assess your progress in learning'
Improve learning and performance: assess learning progress

(W) Words and phrases
add, add on, make it up to, total, altogether, equals, method, check

(r) Resources
for each pair:
two sets of digit cards (0–9)
copy of RS13
wipe boards or sheets of paper and thick pens
copy of RS14 (optional)

Pairs displaying numbers
Each child holds up one part of the number, so that, together, they are showing you a two-digit number.

Mini-plenary
Check whether the ones digits total 10 and the tens digits total 9. If they do, the numbers total 100. If not, a digit has been changed.

For example: "In the equation '26 + 84 = 100', 6 and 4 makes 10, but 2 and 8 makes 10 rather than 9 – so the equation has been altered."

Introduction

Give each pair of children two sets of digit cards. Present the class with a two-digit number. Children work in pairs to find the number which, when added to yours, makes 100 and then display that number.

$$64 + ? = 100$$

Ask one or more of the children how they worked out the answer. If appropriate, model their solutions on an empty number line.

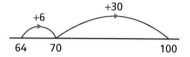

(m) *If you start with 64, how do you work out what to add to make it up to 100? What do you do first?*

(m) *Is there another method that works?*

Pairs

Give each pair a copy of RS13. Children take turns to make a two-digit number with their digit cards, lay these on RS13 and write the correct number in the box to complete the equation. They leave the cards in position until there are eight cards on the sheet.

Child A then closes their eyes, while Child B swaps round two of the cards. Child A opens their eyes, looks at the numbers and says what has been done and how they know this. They replace the cards, explaining why the equations are now correct.

Pairs then swap roles.

After a while, stop the class for a brief discussion of how children work out which cards have been swapped.

(m) *What do those two tens numbers add up to?*

(👥) *How do you know which cards were swapped?*

(😊) *Are you getting any quicker at adding two-digit numbers?*

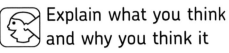
Support: Children use the empty number line to find the number to complete the equation. Child B simply removes one card, and their partner identifies the missing number.

Extend: Children work with RS14 and three-digit numbers that make 500.

Plenary

Pairs of children work in groups of four. Children agree two two-digit numbers that total 100, and each child writes one of these digits on their wipe board.

Invite one group of four to the front to display their numbers.

| 2 | 3 | 7 | 7 |

The rest of the class close their eyes. The four at the front quickly change one digit. The class look and decide which digit has changed, giving reasons.

Repeat this with other groups.

Check whether the class think they have improved their skills.

If I gave you one number ending in 7, what would you look for in the other number?

Now, how would you tackle pairs of numbers that make 100?

> **Preparing for the plenary**
> Use the mini-plenary to remind children to be prepared to present their ideas in the main plenary.

Assessment for learning

Can the children

Find what to add to 47, 29 or 63 to make them up to 100?

Explain why adding the ones and then the tens helps in checking totals for 100?

Say whether they are becoming more confident and accurate at finding and checking these totals?

If not

Do more work with children on using the empty number line.

Ask children who are able to explain this to do so (see 'Peer tutoring', p8). Then ask the child to repeat the explanation they have just heard.

Do some timed tests in which children mark their own score, then practise that area of maths and are re-tested a week later. This gives children more practice in thinking about their own progress.

Adding three small numbers
Classroom technique: Tell your partner

Learning objectives

Maths
Add several small numbers

Speaking and listening
'Explain what you think and why you think it'
Explain and justify thinking

Personal skills
'Think about what you have learned'
Improve learning and performance: reflect on learning

Words and phrases
add, add on, make it up to, total, altogether, equals, strategy, method, explain, check

Resources
display copy of RS15
copies of RS16
for each pair:
copy of RS15
1–6, 0–9 and 1–12 dice
counters in two different colours (see-through if available)

Introduction

Revise with the class some techniques for adding three small numbers.

Display RS15 and introduce a game, in which you are playing against the class. The aim is to cover three numbers in a line.

Roll three dice (1–6, 0–9 and 1–12) and read out the numbers. Children discuss in pairs how they would add two or three of the numbers to make one of the numbers on RS15.

One child gives their answer and an explanation of how they reached it. Cross this number through.

Now roll the dice for yourself and talk through your own addition (again, use two or three of the dice numbers). Circle this number.

Continue until you or the class have a line of three circles or crosses. Award that team a point. A complete game consists of playing like this until one team has three points.

m *What are the possible totals with these dice?*

S *What's the best way of adding these three numbers? Why?*

Tell your partner
This involves all children in thinking about how to add the numbers and prepares them for doing the same in the game they will play later with their partners.

Pairs

Give each pair a copy of RS15. Pairs play the game, using 'Tell your partner' (p11).

m *How could you get that 21 with three dice?*

S *How many ways did you try those three dice?*

☺ *What do you look for now when you see the three dice?*

Tell your partner
The child whose turn it is rolls the dice and decides whether to add two or three of the numbers. They explain their addition. This helps them focus on the procedure they are using, and their partner can check that the calculation is correct.

Support: Give children three 1–6 dice and a copy of RS16.

Extend: Children find totals that can be achieved more frequently.
They can redesign the board so that 'easy' numbers are in the middle.

Plenary

Roll two or three dice and, again, ask children to talk to their partners about how they would add the numbers. Write up suggested strategies.

> **Adding small numbers**
> Look for a pair that makes 10.
> Start with the biggest number.
> Start with 9 because it's easy to add on to.

Reflect on learning
Keep the list of strategies on display for a week or two so that, when you are working with addition, children can try one of the strategies with which they are less familiar.

Children talk to their partner about which strategies they can use confidently, and why.

m *Which are the easiest pairs to deal with?*

Explain why you switched those numbers round first.

Have you developed any new ways of calculating today?

Assessment for learning

Can the children

m Roll the three dice and add the numbers?

Explain how they add three numbers?

Identify strategies from the list that they do and don't use?

If not

m Check whether children are confident with number bonds to 10 + 10. Do more games and activities involving adding numbers, focusing on a variety of strategies.

Add three numbers out loud yourself and ask children to repeat back what you did.

Make a point of asking children to use particular strategies when adding numbers and to name the strategies they use.

Solving money problems
Classroom technique: 1, 2, 3, 4

Learning objectives

m Maths
Use addition to solve problems involving money

Speaking and listening
'Share ideas and reach agreement'
Share and discuss ideas and reach consensus

Personal skills
'Organise your results'
Organise work: organise findings

W Words and phrases
add, add on, make it up to, total, altogether, equals, strategy, method, explain, check

r Resources
display copy of RS17
display calculator
for each group:
copy of RS17
coins (optional)

Thumbs down
This is a variation of 'Devil's advocate' (p11). Looking out for your error keeps children alert. The number of thumbs that are down indicates to you how many children have spotted the error.

1, 2, 3
Tell the children that you will be using this technique in the plenary, as a reminder to share the work and their understanding of it.

Solving the problem
It may not be necessary to add the costs of the three meals – for example, if all the totals are under £1.50, children know that £5 will cover the costs.

U&A Suggest extensions
If groups complete their work confidently and in good time, ask them to extend the problem: "What could we try next?"

Introduction

Display RS17 to the class.

Choose two items from the menu. Individual children add the prices together, then turn to a neighbour and say how they worked this out.

Tell the class that you are going to make a deliberate mistake, then add the same two items yourself, out loud. Ask children to spot the point at which you err, putting their thumb down quietly when they do so.

Invite a child to explain your mistake to the class and help you put it right.

m *What is a useful way to add 99p?*

☺ *How shall I record this calculation on the board?*

Groups of three

Children work in groups of three. Each child chooses two items from the menu and works out their total. They check these totals and work out whether £5 is enough to cover the cost of all three meals.

m *How will you start solving this problem?*

m *Can you estimate the answer, roughly?*

☒ *What are you each doing in your group?*

☺ *How can you organise your recording?*

Support: Provide coins for children to model their calculations with.

Extend: Children choose three items each, combine the total costs as above and work out the change from £10.

Plenary

Using the calculator
This is an opportunity to introduce and practise basic calculator skills. If children are familiar with using a calculator, they check the calculations themselves.

The groups present their work to the class. Choose one member of a group to explain the problem and solution, using '1, 2, 3' (p12). Check each calculation using the display calculator, talking through the key presses with the class as you go along.

 *How will you add these two amounts?*

 *What change would you get from this?*

 *How do you read the display on the calculator?*

 *Is there another way to do that?*

Assessment for learning

Can the children

 Add two amounts of money quickly and accurately, without using coins?

 Say whether they agree with others in their group, and why, or why not?

 Record their work and explain how this record represents their solution?

If not

 Do some work on this, using place value boards to emphasise the value of the digits.

 Check that the level of work is right for the children. It may be that children need to listen more carefully. In this case, ask one child to repeat their opinion, then ask the other two to say whether they agree or disagree.

 Use a model of effective recording (either another group's or your own) to demonstrate the value of organising findings carefully.

Self and peer assessment

Name _____

Lesson 9: Using known number facts	I think	My partner thinks
(m) I can use one addition fact to make some free facts.		
I can repeat how somebody else has explained their calculation.		
I share work with my partner.		

Lesson 10: Number pairs to 100	I think	My partner thinks
(m) I know what to add to 63 to make it up to 100.		
I can explain how I know that 34 and 65 don't total 100.		
I can add pairs that make 100 quickly.		

Name _____

Lesson 11: Adding three small numbers	I think	My partner thinks
(m) I can add three small numbers.		
(💬) I can explain different ways.		
(😊) I know which strategies I like to use when adding three small numbers.		

Lesson 12: Solving money problems	I think	My partner thinks
(m) I can add two amounts of money quickly and accurately.		
(💬) I say something when I don't agree with what someone in my group says.		
(😊) I can organise the way I record calculations.		

Self and peer assessment

Multiplication and division

Learning objectives

	Lessons 13	14	15	16
ⓜ Maths objectives				
recognise multiples in the 2, 3, 4, 5 and 10 multiplication tables	●			
understand the operation of multiplication		●		
begin to know the number facts for the 6, 7, 8 and 9 multiplication tables			●	
carry out a mathematical investigation				●
Ⓢ Speaking and listening skills				
explain and justify thinking	●			
share and discuss ideas and reach consensus		●		
contribute to small-group discussion			●	
reach a common understanding with a partner				●
Personal skills				
work with others: show awareness and understanding of others' needs	●		●	
organise work: use different approaches to tackle a problem		●		
organise work: plan ways to solve a problem				●

About these lessons

Lesson 13: Multiples of numbers

 Recognise multiples in the 2, 3, 4, 5 and 10 multiplication tables

Children not only need to know the number facts in the multiplication tables, they also need to develop a feel for the tables in which the various products appear. This activity helps children develop this broader familiarity with multiples and the relationships between them.

 Explain and justify thinking

Classroom technique: Tell your partner

Children share a task, working out which number from a set of multiples is the 'odd one out' and setting similar problems for another pair. The knowledge that, in the plenary, they may be called on to offer an explanation to the whole class encourages true sharing of ideas.

 Work with others: show awareness and understanding of others' needs

In constructing problems for others to do, children are asked to think about how it would feel to be trying to solve these problems themselves.

Lesson 15: Devising a number puzzle

 Begin to know number facts for the 6, 7, 8 and 9 multiplication tables

Children work out the facts in these tables to construct puzzles for other children to solve, and they, in turn, solve puzzles set by other children. Using the facts in these ways, children become more familiar with them.

 Contribute to small-group discussion

Classroom technique: Think, pair, share

Individuals briefly think in silence about each problem before sharing their ideas with a partner. They then combine forces with another pair to discuss their ideas further.

 Work with others: show awareness and understanding of others' needs

In constructing puzzles for others to do, children have to think about the level of difficulty of the puzzle they are working on and imagine how they would solve it themselves.

Lesson 14: Multiplication strategies

 Understand the operation of multiplication

These problems encourage children to focus on several important aspects of multiplication: the commutative law, the distributive law and the idea that multiplication can be treated as repeated addition. Although the task uses a calculator, the procedures that children develop can increase their repertoire of mental strategies.

 Share and discuss ideas and reach consensus

Classroom technique: Think, pair, share

Individuals briefly think in silence about each calculation before sharing ideas with a partner. They then combine forces with another pair to discuss their ideas further and agree on acceptable methods for solving the problems.

 Organise work: use different approaches to tackle a problem

Looking for alternative methods encourages children to analyse the problems they are dealing with and to develop strategies for simplifying and breaking down the calculations. These same strategies are also useful when working mentally or using informal pencil-and-paper calculations.

Lesson 16: A multiplication investigation

 Carry out a mathematical investigation

Mathematical investigation is a more open-ended process than problem solving and can be daunting unless the activity is structured. That structure is what this lesson provides. This type of structure could be used as a way of starting investigations with other mathematical content.

 Reach a common understanding with a partner

Classroom technique: Peer tutoring

In this activity, children who have poor organisational skills are supported and 'taught' by children who are confident in this area. Together, they take responsibility for the progress of their work, led by the child who acts as 'tutor'.

 Organise work: plan ways to solve a problem

Using the introduction to the lesson to model solving a problem helps children when they come to tackle a similar problem independently later on in the lesson.

Multiples of numbers
Classroom technique: Tell your partner

Learning objectives

m **Maths**
Recognise multiples in the 2, 3, 4, 5 and 10 multiplication tables

Speaking and listening
'Explain what you think and why you think it'
Explain and justify thinking

Personal skills
'Think about what other people need'
Work with others: show awareness and understanding of others' needs

W **Words and phrases**
product, multiple, multiplication grid, set, explain, justify

r **Resources**
display copies of RS18 and RS19
number fans or wipe boards for each pair:
copy of RS19

Tell your partner
Give children a moment to think about this alone, then a short time to discuss it with their partner.

Odd one out
18 7 20 8
"18 and 20 and 8 are in the 2 multiplication table, but 7 isn't."

Showing awareness of others' needs
Match each pair with another of similar ability. In thinking about the other pair, they should record neatly, but make the problems challenging.

Explain and justify
Tell children that they may be asked in the plenary to explain not only the solution to a problem but also how they arrived there.

Introduction

Display the top half of RS18 to the class, with the answers hidden. Have RS19 available to display, if necessary, during the session.

Read out the first set of numbers. Children discuss in pairs which multiplication table the numbers come from and hold up number fans or wipe boards to show you their answer.

Go through the rest of the sequences of numbers on the top half of RS18. Match the line of numbers to the table number. The children will notice that some sets of numbers occur in more than one table.

Now display the second half of RS18. Tell the children that each of these sets of four numbers contains an odd one out that does not belong in that table. Pairs identify both the table and the odd one out and explain how they know this.

m *What patterns do you look for?*

Explain why 21 is the odd one out.

Pairs

Now ask the pairs to work together to produce five sets of multiples (sticking to the 2, 3, 4, 5 or 10 multiplication tables). Each set should have four numbers, one of which is an odd one out.

When they have compiled a list of number sets, ask the children to swap them with another pair and solve each other's problems.

m *In which multiplication tables does that number appear?*

Explain what you mean about spotting odd numbers.

How could you make the odd ones out harder to spot?

Support: Restrict children to just three tables such as the 3, 4 and 5 multiplication tables.

Extend: Concentrate on the 6, 7, 8 and 9 multiplication tables.

Plenary

Pairs present one set of numbers they worked on. Write these up.

> 27   35   81   90

The rest of the class work in pairs to identify the odd one out, using 'Heads or tails' (p12).

Look at a 1–50 grid and mark any numbers that children don't recognise as multiples of any other number.

Odd one out

Children will begin to spot prime numbers, although they won't be sure about numbers beyond 10 times the table number, such as 39. Encourage children who know to explain to the class.

(m) *How many multiplication tables does that number appear in?*

(m) *Tell me some numbers that appear in none of the tables.*

(S) *Why do you say 17 must be the odd one out?*

Assessment for learning

Can the children

(m) Recognise whether a number appears in the 2, 3, 4, 5 or 10 multiplication table?

(S) Say how they decide which number is the odd one out?

(☺) Name one thing that they need to consider when preparing work for another pair?

If not

(m) Do more activities and games using multiples and factors. Count in multiples, using a number line.

(S) Encourage children to check, using a multiplication grid.

(☺) Ask children what is important in the work presented to them: neatness and size of writing, difficulty of problem, number of problems, and so on.

Multiplication strategies
Classroom technique: Think, pair, share

Think, pair, share
Children briefly think about this on their own before turning to a neighbour and sharing their ideas with them.

Introduction

Write up '33 × 7'. Explain that you want to do this calculation on your calculator, but the 'x' key is broken. Take suggestions.

m *What does '33 multiplied by 7' mean?*

m *Why is '33 multiplied by 7' the same as '33 plus 33 plus 33' …?*

☺ *Is there another way to solve this problem?*

Pairs/Groups of four

Present four further calculations to the class.

86 × 3	102 × 4	91 × 4	84 × 5

Give each pair of children a calculator. Each pair works together to record a way of doing each calculation, without using the 'x' key.

After ten minutes, pairs join with another pair and share and compare solutions. They discuss alternative ways of doing the calculations.

Children then spend a further few minutes in their original pairs, recording different way of doing each calculation.

m *Why does adding work here?*

⟲ *Do you agree with what Jamie has just said? Why not?*

☺ *Suppose you did this calculation without a calculator. What would you do?*

Support: Help children model each stage of their calculation on an empty number line.

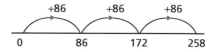

Extend: Replace 3, 4 and 5 in the multiplications with 6, 7 or 8. Children prepare an explanation of why each of their solutions works.

Learning objectives

m Maths
Understand the operation of multiplication

Speaking and listening
'Share ideas and reach agreement'
Share and discuss ideas and reach consensus

Personal skills
'Try different way to tackle a problem'
Organise work: use different approaches to tackle a problem

w Words and phrases
times, product, multiplied by, repeated addition, calculation, method, jotting, operation, symbol, equation

r Resources
display calculator for each pair/group: calculators

Using the 'x' key
There is no reason why children should not use the 'x' key to find out or check the answer. The challenge here is not to find the answer, but to find a different way to reach that answer.

Difficult or easy?
Some children will do the calculations mentally. Focusing on methods for solving easy problems allows children to see how to use the same strategies with other problems.

Alternative methods
Children will need to think about strategies for simplifying each calculation.

Plenary

With the class, go over each calculation in turn. For each calculation, establish a solution based on repeated addition of the larger number.

Preparing for the plenary
Observe groups and pairs and identify any whom you would like to present a particular idea in the plenary. Tell these children in advance that they may be asked to talk to the class.

$$86 + 86 + 86 = 258$$
$$102 + 102 + 102 + 102 = 408$$
$$91 + 91 + 91 + 91 = 364$$
$$84 + 84 + 84 + 84 + 84 = 420$$

Collect in alternative solutions, together with explanations, from the children whom you identified earlier.

"For 102×4, four hundreds are 400, and two fours are 8, so just add 400 and 8."

"For 84×5, you can multiply 84 by 10 in your head, then halve it."

(m) *Why does that method work?*

(s) *Tell your partner how you would use Carol's method for doing 62×5.*

(☺) *Does anyone have another way of doing 84×5?*

Assessment for learning

Can the children

(m) Find the answer to 86×3 without using multiplication?

(s) Share and compare solutions?

(☺) Find an alternative method of their own, or use someone else's, to reach an answer?

If not

(m) Use a range of models such as rectangular grids, number line, sets of objects, calculators, and so on. Children may not have a broad understanding of what multiplication is all about.

(s) Use 'Think, pair, share' (p10) for a range of contexts in case children find this way of working difficult.

(☺) Do some work on modelling this with grids, as children may not understand the distributive nature of multiplication – for example, that 4×12 equals 4×10 plus 4×2.

Devising a number puzzle
Classroom technique: Think, pair, share

Learning objectives

(m) Maths
Begin to know number facts for the 6, 7, 8 and 9 multiplication tables

Speaking and listening
'Join in a discussion with a small group'
Contribute to small-group discussion

Personal skills
'Think about what other people need'
Work with others: show awareness and understanding of others' needs

(W) Words and phrases
times, product, multiply, calculate, calculation, method, jotting, operation, symbol, equation, answer, solution

(r) Resources
display copy of RS20
for each pair:
copy of RS20
copy of RS21 (optional)
copy of RS19 (optional)
calculators (optional)
digit cards (optional)

Think, pair, share
Give children one minute on their own, another minute to discuss with a partner and a further minute for two pairs to talk together about their ideas and solutions.

Support
Some children may prefer to use the 'cloud' model for an unknown number, as used on RS21.

Showing awareness of others' needs
Ask children to think about how difficult the problems they devise are and ask them to grade each problem: 'H' (for 'Hard'), 'E' (for 'Easy') or 'M' (for 'Medium'). Explain that, when it comes to solving the problems, children can choose ones that suit their level of confidence and knowledge.

Using known number facts to find unknown ones
Remind children that they can use facts they know to work out ones they don't know – for example, repeated doubling as a way to multiply by 4 or 8.

Introduction

Display the first section of RS20. Write the number '11' in the first box and the number '30' in the second box.

Children try to find the mystery numbers.

Invite one or two children to give their solutions and to talk about how they found them. Write these up.

$$6 + 5 = 11$$
$$6 \times 5 = 30$$

(m) *How did you know that the two numbers weren't 10 and 1?*

(m) *How can you work out five sixes if you don't know the 6 times table yet?*

Pairs

Give each pair of children a copy of RS20. Pairs work together to devise further problems of their own, following the same format but substituting different numbers. Explain that these problems will be given to another pair to solve. Children use the numbers 6, 7, 8 and 9 in some, if not all, of their problems.

(m) *How can you check that you've got those numbers right?*

(speaking) *How can you use doubling to help you multiply 6 by 8?*

(personal) *I wonder why you classed that problem as 'E' for 'Easy'?*

Support: Provide digit cards for children to place on the clouds on RS21. Children use a multiplication grid (RS19) or a calculator to find facts they don't know.

Extend: Using higher numbers, children work mentally or with jottings, rather than with multiplication grids or calculators.

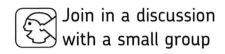 Join in a discussion with a small group

Plenary

Collect in the children's work and choose at least one problem of each level of difficulty ('H', 'M' and 'E') to write up. The 'cloud' format used on RS23 is a quick way of doing this.

Groups of four agree a problem that they want to work on, using the 'Think, pair, share' technique (p10).

Sharing
Make sure that groups work on problems devised by pairs outside their group.

Briefly discuss strategies with the class.

m *If this number is 7, what does that one have to be?*

m *Will the multiplication answer always be bigger than the addition answer?*

↻ *Talk to your group about how you start solving one of these problems.*

Assessment for learning

Can the children
m Mentally find out a number fact from the 6, 7, 8 or 9 multiplication tables?

↻ Stay silent while another child is talking?

☺ Say whether the puzzle they invented is easy, medium or hard to solve?

If not
m Do some work on using known multiplication facts to derive unknown ones – for example, doubling to get from 6×2 to 6×8 or from 3×3 to 3×6.

↻ Use a 'talking stick' (p10) to formalise children's roles of 'Speaker' and 'Listener'. Make sure that listeners are taking in what is said by occasionally asking them to repeat what was just said by another child.

☺ Ask the child to imagine what it would be like for someone solving their puzzle who did not know many multiplication facts or for someone who knew all of them up to 10×10.

A multiplication investigation
Classroom technique: Peer tutoring

Being systematic
First record the multiplications in any order, then model systematic working by putting them in order to check you have found all the products. Cross out any repeats and write out the six products as a list.

1 2 3 4

  2 3 4 6 8 12

1: 1×2 1×3 1×4

2: 2×1 2×3 2×3

3: 3×1 3×2 3×4

4: 4×1 4×2 4×3

Investigating
Changing just one aspect of a problem generates new ideas to investigate which are manageable for children, because they are not too different from the original.

Peer tutoring
Try to pair children so that one of each pair is organised and can work systematically. You may need to put some children in groups of three.

Introduction

Invite four children to hold up one of the large digit cards. Then ask two of these children at a time to hold up their numbers and agree the product of these two numbers. Work with the class to find all the different products that can be made by multiplying two of the numbers together. (There are six possible products.)

Briefly discuss with the children anything they notice about the results.

Go over with the children what this problem asked them to do and write up their explanations. Discuss and record some ways in which a different problem can be created by changing just one feature at a time.

This problem	Change it to
Multiplying two numbers	Multiplying three numbers Subtracting, adding or dividing two numbers
There are four numbers.	Use three or five numbers.
The numbers are 1, 2, 3, 4.	Use four other single-digit numbers. Use two-digit numbers.

(m) *Jack says that all the answers except for one are even. Why is that?*

(S&L) *Talk to your partner about why being systematic helps us check we have found all the products.*

Pairs

On the board, write up the original problem: "Here are four digits: 1, 2, 3, 4. Find all the products you can make by multiplying two of these digits together."

Children work in pairs to think of one way to change this problem. Emphasise that they should keep all other aspects of the problem the same. Take a few examples to make sure children understand what you mean. Then ask them to write out this new problem in words before exploring and answering it.

(m) *You are multiplying three numbers and keeping everything else the same. So put into words the problem you are investigating.*

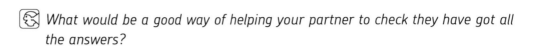

What would be a good way of helping your partner to check they have got all the answers?

What can you do first? What do you need to know first?

Support: Set children the same problem as the original, but with any four digits they choose.

Extend: Provide calculators to support adventurous children who are working beyond their knowledge base – for example, multiplying large numbers or several small numbers.

Plenary

A few pairs present and talk about their work.

Other pairs pin up their work on an 'Ideas board' (p13), where it can be seen by the class over the next few days.

You did two investigations. Which was more interesting, and why?

Tell us how you set about solving that problem.

Assessment for learning

Can the children

Choose one way to change the original problem and solve this new problem?

Say, at any point in their investigation, where they have got to?

Explain what they will do first to 'enter' the problem?

If not

Work on 'finding all the possibilities' problems as children may need more experience of working systematically.

Suggest that children use 'One between two' (p8) to share a pencil. This technique requires children to pay close attention to each other's processes in a shared problem.

Focus on problem solving with the class and discuss useful strategies for entering, solving and checking problems.

Self and peer assessment

Lesson 13: Multiples of numbers	I think	My partner thinks
(m) I can say whether 18 or 24 appears in any of these multiplication tables: 2, 3, 4, 5 or 10.		
I can work out which number in a set of multiples doesn't belong there.		
I can record work for others to read.		

Lesson 14: Multiplication strategies	I think	My partner thinks
(m) I can find the answer to 86 × 3.		
I share my solutions with my partner.		
I can use two different methods to reach an answer to a multiplication problem.		

Name _____

Lesson 15: Devising a number puzzle	I think	My partner thinks
(m) I can remember or work out any fact from the 6, 7, 8 or 9 multiplication tables.		
I listen while my partner is talking.		
I can invent an easy, medium or hard puzzle for the right person.		

Lesson 16: A multiplication investigation	I think	My partner thinks
(m) I can think of a way to change the original problem.		
I can say where we got to with our investigation.		
I think about what to do first when solving a problem.		

Self and peer assessment

Handling data

Learning objectives

	Lessons			
	17	**18**	**19**	**20**
ⓜ Maths objectives				
organise data on a Venn diagram	●			
organise and represent data on a Carroll diagram		●		
extract data from tables			●	
interpret data in bar charts				●
Ⓢ Speaking and listening skills				
explain and justify thinking	●		●	
contribute to whole-class discussion		●		
contribute to small-group discussion				●
☺ Personal skills				
improve learning and performance: develop confidence in own judgements	●			
work with others: give feedback sensitively		●		
improve learning and performance: take pride in work			●	
work with others: work cooperatively with others				●

About these lessons

Lesson 17: Venn diagrams

 Organise data on a Venn diagram

Children sort numbers onto a Venn diagram showing two intersecting sets. This allows them to explore relationships between numbers, such as the fact that any number which is a multiple of 2 and of 3 is also a multiple of 6 or that numbers ending in 1 are never multiples of 5.

 Explain and justify thinking

Classroom technique: Heads or tails

Pairs of children formulate statements about their discoveries, knowing that either of them may be called on to give their explanations in the plenary – so both must take equal responsibility for understanding these explanations.

 Improve learning and performance: develop confidence in own judgements

Choosing their own properties to sort by allows children to work at a level at which they feel comfortable and helps them develop confidence in the results of their sorting.

Lesson 18: Carroll diagrams

 Organise and represent data on a Carroll diagram

Representing shapes on a Carroll diagram works at two levels: it helps children understand how these diagrams work and allows them to see connections between apparently diverse shapes.

 Contribute to whole-class discussion

Classroom technique: Think, pair, share

Children think about where their shape belongs, then share their ideas with a partner and, finally, combine forces with another pair to review their completed work. The discussion that ensues gives children ideas that they can later share during the class discussion in the plenary session.

 Work with others: give feedback sensitively

In the plenary, children turn to their partner and say one thing they have enjoyed about working together on the task. Warning children in advance that this will happen encourages them to think during the lesson about what they themselves are like to work with.

Lesson 19: Tally charts

 Extract data from tables

In this lesson, children interpret a tally chart showing a sorcerer's stocktake to answer questions about his goods.

 Explain and justify thinking

Classroom technique: Heads or tails

Both partners prepare themselves to offer their explanation to the class in the plenary, because neither child knows who will win the toss of the coin.

 Improve learning and performance: take pride in work

Children are encouraged to review their work and to identify aspects of it about which they can feel proud.

Lesson 20: Bar charts

 Interpret data in bar charts

Children play a game in which they record the roll of a dice on a version of a bar chart. This is made interesting by considering how to represent the dice rolls unfairly so that one particular number wins. In the process, children need to think about the difference between correct and incorrect ways of recording on a bar chart.

 Contribute to small-group discussion

Classroom technique: Talking stick

With pairs working in groups of four, children take turns to explain and discuss their ideas with the aid of a 'talking stick'. The stick ensures that children are listened to attentively and without interruption.

 Work with others: work cooperatively with others

Children share tasks first with a partner, then a group of four. The context of a game engages children, encouraging cooperation.

Venn diagrams

Classroom technique: Heads or tails

Learning objectives

(m) Maths
Organise data on
a Venn diagram

Speaking and listening
'Explain what you think
and why you think it'
Explain and justify thinking

Personal skills
'Develop confidence
about what you think
and decide'
Improve learning and
performance: develop
confidence in own judgements

(W) Words and phrases
multiple, property,
record, data, Venn diagram,
label, explain, generalise,
predict, check

(r) Resources
display copy of RS22
for each pair:
copy of RS22
100-square

Tell your partner
Children discuss with their
partner whereabouts on the
diagram the number belongs
each time. Ask for suggestions
and check whether the other
children agree or disagree.

Tell your partner
Use this technique again
to discuss the diagram.

Introduction

Display RS22 and brainstorm properties of numbers
for sorting two-digit numbers. List these.

odd	has a 1 in it	multiple of 10
even	has not got	in 3× table ...
ends in 3	a 5 in it	

Choose two of these properties and label the two sets
accordingly. The different parts of the diagram are
also labelled 'A', 'B', 'C' and 'D' to help children refer to
them.

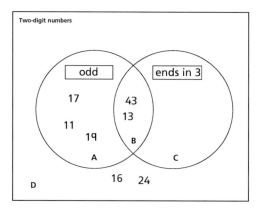

Invite suggestions for two-digit numbers and put these
onto the diagram with the help of the children.

When about ten or twelve numbers have been
sorted, children explain these. Write up the children's
comments and explanations as a model for children's

What?	Why?
There are no numbers in section C	Because numbers that end in 3 are always odd
The numbers in section D will always be even	Because the odd numbers are in sections A and B

paired work, distinguishing between 'whats' and 'whys'.

(m) *What can you say about the numbers in section B
of the diagram?*

*What do the numbers in section D have in
common? How do you work that out?*

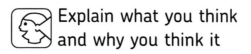
Pairs

Give each pair of children a copy of RS22 to work with, for them to choose their own properties to sort by.

After they have sorted about 20 numbers, children discuss and record an explanation of their results.

Support: Help children choose properties they know about, such as 'even' and 'multiple of 10'. Provide a 100-square as a check.

Extend: Children choose properties so that numbers appear in each part of the diagram or where a specific part is left empty.

Plenary

Pairs present their discoveries, using the 'Heads or tails' technique (p12). Write up a few examples.

 Can you say why there were no numbers in this part of your diagram?

Tell us how you know that must be true.

Choosing numbers
Children test whether each part of their diagram will have numbers to go in it. They may find that one section must remain empty.

Heads or tails
Warn children that you will be using this technique in the plenary. This means that both members of the pair should be prepared to talk about what they have found out from their sorting. Emphasise that you want explanations about 'why', not just descriptions of 'what'.

U&A Testing statements
Encourage children to test their statements by looking for counter-examples: "Can we find a number that is a multiple of both 2 and 3, but is *not* a multiple of 6?"

Assessment for learning

Can the children

Ⓜ Find the correct place on their diagram to write their numbers?

Reach a conclusion about the results of their sorting?

Speak confidently when telling you or the class about their conclusion?

If not

Ⓜ Go back to first principles, sorting number cards into two separated hoops and talking about what to do with the cards that belong in both hoops, as children may not understand the significance of intersection.

Ask children to look at each section of the diagram and describe the numbers there. Make a statement yourself for them to agree or disagree with.

Help children formulate some statements about their sorting and to check each one by looking for counter-examples.

Carroll diagrams
Classroom technique: Think, pair, share

Learning objectives

(m) Maths
Organise and represent data on a Carroll diagram

Speaking and listening
'Join in a discussion with the whole class'
Contribute to whole-class discussion

Personal skills
'Give feedback sensitively'
Work with others: give feedback sensitively

(W) Words and phrases
data, information, diagram, regular, irregular, symmetrical, table, sort, record, organise, represent

(r) Resources
for each pair:
copy of RS23
geostrips

Regular and irregular
Revise these terms and remind children that symmetrical shapes are not necessarily regular.

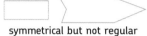

symmetrical but not regular

Keeping shapes for the plenary
Pairs may need to dismantle their shapes in order to make more, so ask children to keep any shapes that you particularly want them to show in the plenary
(aim to have examples for each of the four sections of the Carroll diagram).

Introduction

Display RS23. Explain that the children will work in pairs to make shapes, using geostrips, and record these on a Carroll diagram.

Briefly establish where on this diagram a few shapes (for example, a square and an isosceles triangle) would belong.

Tell children that, in the plenary, they are going to give feedback on how well they worked in pairs.

(m) *Why does the isosceles triangle not go here?*

(s) *Who disagrees about where the pentagon goes? Why?*

Pairs/Groups of four

Give each pair a copy of RS23. Children use geostrips to make a shape and decide which section of the Carroll diagram the shape goes in. They discuss and agree this with their partner and sketch their shapes onto the diagram.

The pair works together to make and draw two shapes in each section of the diagram.

Each pair joins with another pair to compare and check their results.

Support: Help children to focus first on regular and irregular shapes, using a simplified Carroll diagram.

regular	irregular

Extend: Children think about different criteria for the Carroll diagram, such as 'symmetrical or not'.

(m) *What other shapes could you make that belong in both 'four sides' and 'regular'?*

(m) *If you distort that shape, does it still belong in that section?*

Plenary

Focus with the class on each section of the Carroll diagram in turn. Pairs with a shape that belongs in the section under discussion show that shape.

Discuss what else might go in each section.

Pairs tell their partner one thing they have enjoyed about working together in this lesson.

How can we describe the shapes in this section?

Which section seems to have most shapes? Why might that be?

Is there anything you want to add to your partner's feedback?

Assessment for learning

Can the children

Make a shape to put in each section of the Carroll diagram?

Volunteer an idea or comment in the whole-class discussion?

Find something appreciative to say when asked to give feedback?

If not

Concentrate on working with children in the following areas: regular and irregular shapes; sorting by two criteria; or using geostrips.

Note who doesn't contribute to the discussion and make sure they do so on another occasion in a smaller group.

Take suggestions from the class about working positively with a partner.

Tally charts
Classroom technique: Heads or tails

Learning objectives

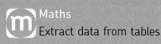 **Maths**
Extract data from tables

Speaking and listening
'Explain what you think and why you think it'
Explain and justify thinking

Personal skills
'Take pride in your work'
Improve learning and performance: take pride in work

Words and phrases
tally, data, represent, table, method, jotting, answer, correct, explain, justify

Resources
display copy of RS24
for each pair:
copy of RS25

Involving the class

Children turn to their neighbour to answer your questions.

Heads or tails

Emphasise that either partner may be called on to explain their reasoning in the plenary, so both must understand their answers.

Preparing for the plenary

Direct children to focus on two or three particular explanations so that when you come to the plenary, you don't end up with 30 children who can answer questions 1 to 5 and no one who has prepared answers to the remaining questions.

Introduction

Introduce the idea of a sorcerer's magic shop, where the sorcerer is doing a stocktake. Remind children about tallying. Display RS24 and, with the class, work out how many of the various items he has in stock. Ask the children questions about the stock.

How many packs of toad warts has he got? And if he opened the packs, how many actual toad warts would he have?

How many grams of moon dust does he have altogether? How do you work it out?

Pairs

Give each pair a copy of RS25. Tell the pairs that they are the sorcerer's apprentices taking a test. They look at each statement on the sheet, decide whether it is true or false and write 'T' or 'F' beside it accordingly. They also will need to explain their reasoning.

What do you need to find out? How can you do that?

Will people understand that explanation?

Which answer are you most pleased with?

Support: Partner less confident children with others who help with 'Peer tutoring' (p8).

Extend: Children add two items (and their quantities) to the stock list, then make up some true and false statements.

Explain what you think
and why you think it

Plenary

Pairs give their answer to one statement, using 'Heads or tails' (p12). Tell the rest of the class to mark their own work.

Children review their work with their partner and identify which part or aspect they feel they have achieved well.

Is there anything else you need to tell the class?

Has anyone got any questions they would like to ask this pair?

Who feels they have worked well on these problems?

Ticket to explain
You could expect children to re-explain the reasoning of the last child before giving their own explanation.

Assessment for learning

Can the children

(m) Interpret the tally marks and say how many of each item the sorcerer has in stock?

Explain how they worked out the answer to one of the questions?

Identify something about their work in the lesson that they feel they have done well?

If not

(m) Use tallying with the class to keep track of anything from lost pencils and books borrowed to merit marks.

Ask those children who can explain these questions to do so, then ask the child to repeat the explanation they have just heard.

Ask the child's partner to identify something they think the child did well.

Bar charts
Classroom technique: Talking stick

Learning objectives

(m) **Maths**
Interpret data in bar charts

(speaking icon) **Speaking and listening**
'Join in a discussion with a small group'
Contribute to small-group discussion

(personal icon) **Personal skills**
'Work cooperatively with others'
Work with others: work cooperatively with others

(W) **Words and phrases**
bar chart, most often, least often, probability, likely, unlikely, predict, certain, fair, unfair

(r) **Resources**
display copy of RS26
1–6 dice
for each pair:
copy of RS26
1–6 dice

Introduction

Display the top half of RS26, showing six 'race tracks'. Explain to the class that you will repeatedly roll a dice and each time cross out a square on the track belonging to that number. Allocate the class to teams (from 1 to 6).

Roll the dice and say the number, then cross out the first square on the track of that number. Continue like this.

Who will win?
Make sure the view is put forward that any team could win, because the dice is equally likely to land with any of the six numbers uppermost. However, do not expect all children to grasp this completely.

After a few turns, ask the children to discuss in pairs which team they think will reach the finish first, and why. Have a few more throws, then open out the discussion to the class.

Continue playing. After a while, repeat the question about which team is likely to win, and why. Stop the game when one team has won.

(m) *Which team is doing best so far? Do you think they will win? Why do you think that?*

(m) *Which team is coming second? Last?*

(m) *The dice showed 2 last time. Does that affect whether it shows 2 again this time?*

Pairs/Groups of four

Mini-plenary
When most pairs have finished their game, stop the class briefly and compare which numbers have 'won'. Take the opportunity again to underline that any of the numbers is equally likely to come up.

Give each pair a copy of RS26. Pairs play the same game on the top half of the sheet, crossing out squares as they go along.

Pairs then work together to change the rules of this game to make it *unfair* to one or more teams.

'Talking stick' rules
Give the stick to one child: this child speaks first.
If another child wants to speak, they hold up a finger. When the child with the stick has said as much as they want to, they pass the stick to another child (generally a person who is holding up a finger).
Children listen to the person with the stick and must not interrupt.

After five or ten minutes, pairs combine into groups of four, sharing their ideas for a new game and using a 'talking stick'.

Children then return to their pairs and agree and write down the rules of their game, influenced by their group discussion as they see fit.

Children play their 'unfair' game on the lower section of RS26 to check it works. Suggest that they draw the crosses lightly so these can be rubbed out if they play more than once.

(m) *How can you tell which team is winning?*

(s) *Can you explain how to make this game unfair?*

(☺) *How will you decide which person to give the 'talking stick' to?*

Support: Work with this group.

Extend: Children imagine a race track with 100 spaces on each track rather than ten, thinking about how a 'fair' game on that track might end up.

Plenary

Pairs demonstrate their 'unfair' game to the class on your display version of RS26, talking through their ideas as they do so. Help the class discuss these.

(m) *This pair's idea was to cross out a 6 square every time a 1 came up as well as when a 6 did. Does their chart look as if number 6 came up most?*

(m) *How is this chart unfair?*

(m) *In what way is this game unfair?*

Assessment for learning

Can the children

(m) Interpret the chart?

(s) Contribute to the group discussion when it is their turn to hold the 'talking stick'?

(☺) Take an equal role with their partner in devising an unfair game?

If not

(m) Leave the question of unfairness aside. Go back to the fair version of the game and establish that the children can read that one correctly. If not, work more on this with them.

(s) Ask children to say whether or not they agree with how their partner described their ideas. See if they can talk about whether they think the original version of the game is fair or not.

(☺) Make more use of 'One between two' (p8) to sharpen children's efforts to cooperate.

Name _____

Self and peer assessment

Lesson 17: Venn diagrams	I think	My partner thinks
(m) I can choose two number properties to sort numbers by.		
I can explain the Venn diagram.		
I feel confident about the work I did on sorting numbers.		

Lesson 18: Carroll diagrams	I think	My partner thinks
(m) I can tell when a shape is in the wrong section of the Carroll diagram.		
I sometimes speak in whole-class discussion.		
I can find something to appreciate about working with my partner and can tell them what it is.		

Name _____

Lesson 19: Tally charts	I think	My partner thinks
(m) I can easily work out what the tally marks mean.		
(☒) I can explain how I work out the answer.		
(☺) I can find something about my work in this lesson to feel proud of.		

Lesson 20: Bar charts	I think	My partner thinks
(m) I can read on the bar chart which team is winning a race.		
(☒) I am prepared to take the 'talking stick' when it is offered and say something.		
(☺) I talk with my partner about our work.		

Self and peer assessment

Measures

Learning objectives

	Lessons			
	21	**22**	**23**	**24**
(m) Maths objectives				
use a ruler to measure lines to the nearest half-centimetre	●			
use a ruler accurately and for a purpose		●		
calculate the perimeters of simple shapes			●	
read scales to a suitable level of accuracy				●
Speaking and listening skills				
use precise language to explain ideas or give information	●			●
contribute to whole-class discussion		●		
contribute to small-group discussion			●	
Personal skills				
improve learning and performance: critically evaluate own work	●			
work with others: show awareness and understanding of others' needs		●		●
improve learning and performance: develop confidence in own judgements			●	

About these lessons

Lesson 21: Measuring shapes

 Use a ruler to measure lines to the nearest half-centimetre

Adding an element of challenge and competition to the measuring of lines can lift a simple exercise and help engage children with it.

 Use precise language to explain ideas or give information

Classroom technique: Barrier game

In this activity, children cannot see each other's sheet of shapes. One child places a counter on a shape and measures a dimension of the shape. The first child tells their partner what this measurement is, so that they can put a counter on the same shape on their sheet.

 Improve learning and performance: critically evaluate own work

The plenary of this lesson is given over to a review of the maths objectives and the speaking and listening objectives for this lesson. There is also an evaluation of how well children met these objectives working in pairs.

Lesson 22: Designing a ruler

 Use a ruler accurately and for a purpose

Using a ruler for a real purpose (that of making another ruler for a younger child) requires children to measure accurately and helps them develop a secure understanding of the concepts and techniques involved.

 Contribute to whole-class discussion

Classroom technique: Talking partners

Sharing a task with a partner and talking over ideas with them allows children to rehearse what they say in a discussion involving the whole class.

 Work with others: show awareness and understanding of others' needs

Making a ruler for a younger child means that children must put themselves in that younger child's shoes and consider what their abilities and needs might be.

Lesson 23: Perimeters of shapes

 Calculate the perimeters of simple shapes

In this activity, children discuss whether statements about the perimeters of shapes are true. This gets them thinking about and calculating the perimeters of various simple shapes.

 Contribute to small-group discussion

Classroom technique: Devil's advocate

Statements – false or ambiguous as well as true – can be better than questions at provoking discussion. In this lesson, children are presented with statements with which they can choose to agree or disagree. Working as a group, children argue for or against a statement, with the aim of reaching consensus.

 Improve learning and performance: develop confidence in own judgements

Discussion of dubious statements helps children understand the issues behind them and feel confident that they are moving towards a well-thought-out decision.

Lesson 24: Marking weights on a scale

 Read scales to a suitable degree of accuracy

To read scales, children need enough number knowledge to work out the size of the intervals between the markers. This lesson gives children experience of reading scales that will boost both their skills and their confidence.

 Use precise language to explain ideas or give information

Classroom technique: Peer tutoring

Children often make good teachers, because they remember what helped them bridge the gap between ignorance and understanding. To fulfil the role of 'Peer tutor', the child must use language carefully to explain what they know.

 Work with others: show awareness and understanding of others' needs

Each child, when in the role of 'Peer tutor', must think about how to pace the work for their 'Pupils' and how to correct their work in a sensitive way.

Measuring shapes
Classroom technique: Barrier game

Learning objectives

(m) Maths
Use a ruler
to measure lines to the
nearest half-centimetre

(👄) Speaking and listening
'Use precise language
when talking'
Use precise language to explain
ideas or give information

(😊) Personal skills
'Evaluate your own work'
Improve learning and
performance: critically evaluate
own work

(W) Words and phrases
half-centimetre, length,
centre, perimeter, radius,
circumference, diameter,
approximately, roughly,
nearly, near, nearest

(r) Resources
metre rule
for each pair:
two copies of RS27
or RS28
rulers and pencils
compasses and
set squares (optional)

Measuring to the nearest half-centimetre
Many children will have pencils
whose length is not a multiple of
0.5 cm. They will need to judge
whether the length is nearer to,
for example, 10 cm or 10.5 cm.

Tell your partner
Give children a minute to think
about this, then ask them to
share their thoughts with
their partner.

Introduction

Ask the children what is important to bear in mind
when measuring the length of a pencil with a ruler
to the nearest half-centimetre.

Collect in ideas and write them up.

> **Guidelines to use when measuring**
> Start at the zero mark, not the end of the ruler.
> Keep the pencil still.
> The length might not be a number of centimetres.
> You might need to approximate.

Working in pairs, children then measure their pencils
and tell their partner the results.

(m) *Why do you think rulers have an extra bit before
the zero? What happens if you include that extra
bit in your measurement?*

(👄) *Is your pencil exactly 12 centimetres or is it
12 centimetres to the nearest half-centimetre?*

Pairs

Give each child a copy of RS27. Pairs sit back to
back. Child A puts a cross on one of the shapes,
measures one of its dimensions (radius or diameter if
a circle; length if a square) and then tells their partner
what this measurement is: "My line is approximately
5.5 cm in length." Child B uses a ruler to check which
shape fits the description and puts a cross on that
shape. The pair then compares sheets as a check
before rubbing out their crosses and swapping roles.

(m) *Is the length of the line nearer the centimetre mark
or the half-centimetre mark?*

(👄) *What is the difference between 'exactly five
centimetres' and 'approximately five centimetres'?*

(😊) *Are your measuring skills improving?*

Support: Give children RS28 (a simplified version of RS27) to work with.

Extend: Give children compasses, rulers and set squares for them to create a similar sheet for another pair to work with. When drawing a square, suggest that children measure its diagonals rather than its sides. Expect them to measure to the nearest millimetre.

Plenary

Pairs discuss how well they think they did at

- using a ruler to measure lines;
- using precise language when talking.

(m) *If I say this pencil is about 12 cm long, what might it measure exactly?*

How would you explain to someone over the phone how to use a ruler?

Is there an aspect of measuring lines that you need to improve?

Giving feedback

Child A has a minute to say how they think they did. Child B then endorses what Child A has said or adds their own view. Repeat this process, starting with Child B.

Assessment for learning

Can the children

(m) Measure lines to the nearest half-centimetre?

Use the words 'radius', 'diameter', 'approximately', 'nearly', 'roughly' in appropriate ways?

Find one thing they did well in the lesson and one thing they need to improve?

If not

(m) Use the 'guidelines' drawn up in the lesson to assess which aspect of measuring is causing problems and address this in direct teaching.

Have a 'word of the week' and focus on using it frequently in context with the children.

Suggest specific points for the children to consider: "Did you start at the zero rather than at the end of the ruler?"; "Did you explain clearly which shape you had marked with a cross so that your partner could understand you?"

Designing a ruler
Classroom technique: Talking partners

Learning objectives

(m) Maths
Use a ruler accurately and for a purpose

Speaking and listening
'Join in a discussion with the whole class'
Contribute to whole-class discussion

Personal skills
'Think about what other people need'
Work with others: show awareness and understanding of others' needs

(W) Words and phrases
length, width, height, centimetre, half-centimetre, interval, measure, accurate

(r) Resources
for each pair:
rulers and pencils
sheets of A4 paper and card, each cut into four strips lengthways

Introduction

Explain to the class that they are each going to design and make a ruler for a Year 2 child. Establish that, in Year 2, children are expected to be able to measure to the nearest whole centimetre, but some of them may be able to work with half-centimetres.

Brainstorm with the class things for which Year 2 children might use rulers. Write up ideas.

> how long a book is
> how big a square is
> the depth of water in a flask
> how tall a plant is

Tell your partner
Give children a minute or two to talk with their partner. Then take suggestions from the class.

Children then look at their own rulers and think about ways in which they could simplify these for Year 2 children to use. (Use 'Tell your partner', p11.) Collect in and discuss the children's ideas.

What would be the advantages of showing half-centimetres? And the disadvantages?

Would Year 2 children be able to measure with a ruler like yours?

Pairs

Children work in pairs. Give each child a strip of A4 paper and ask them to design a ruler for Year 2 children, bearing in mind the issues discussed earlier.

Then give each child a strip of card to make the final version of the ruler.

Preparing for the plenary
Ask children to note any difficulties or other issues that arise during their task, to talk about in the plenary.

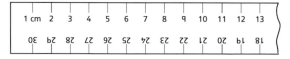

How can you use your existing ruler to mark the centimetres on the ruler that you are making?

Tell me why you chose to write in only the even numbers.

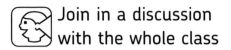
Support: Have some examples available of rulers marked in centimetres and half-centimetres, without a dead end.

Extend: Children invent some lines for Year 2 children to measure, either an exact number of centimetres or half-centimetres, and note down the answers.

Plenary

Have a class discussion about the decisions that the children made and the difficulties of making an accurate tool such as a ruler.

(m) *I wonder who had problems marking where the centimetre lines should go?*

(🗣) *Does everyone agree with what Kylie just said? Does anyone disagree?*

(😊) *Did anyone else choose to colour the spaces between alternate markers? Why did you make that decision?*

Optional follow-up
Arrange a session where your class can work with the Year 2 class and teach the children how to use their rulers.

Who speaks and who doesn't?
Ask for a show of hands from children who did not offer a contribution. Jot down their initials and explain that next time you have a class discussion, you will make sure they get a turn to speak.

Assessment for learning

Can the children

(m) Use a ruler to make marks at intervals of 1 cm on the card ruler they are making?

(🗣) Volunteer a comment in whole-class discussion?

(😊) Give reasons for the choices they made about the ruler they have designed, in the context of the needs of a Year 2 child?

If not

(m) Give children practice in using a ruler for drawing lines of a specified length, making sure that they keep the ruler still.

(🗣) Make sure children are given opportunities to speak in a smaller group. Prompt children with focused questions if necessary.

(😊) Provide more experience for children to imagine themselves in others' positions through simple drama activities or story writing.

Perimeters of shapes
Classroom technique: Devil's advocate

Learning objectives

m **Maths**
Calculate the perimeters of simple shapes

Speaking and listening
'Join in a discussion with a small group'
Contribute to small-group discussion

Personal skills
'Develop confidence about what you think and decide'
Improve learning and performance: develop confidence in own judgements

w **Words and phrases**
length, width, height, centimetre, measure, edge, perimeter, circumference, square, triangle, hexagon, rectangle, circle, regular

r **Resources**
display copy of RS29
for each group:
cards cut from RS29
rulers and pencils

RS29 statement cards

A impossible
B possible
C impossible
D possible
E impossible
F impossible
G possible
H possible

Devil's advocate

In this activity, no one is actually arguing for the false statements (although if children are able and willing to do so, encourage them to). Just being presented with simple statements of contentious ideas provides material for discussion and clarification.

Introduction

Display RS29 and read through the list of words with the class. Briefly revise the idea of 'perimeter' and check that children can read and understand other words on the list, such as 'rectangle' or 'hexagon'. Working in groups of three, children discuss any meanings that they are unclear about.

In your group, talk about what 'perimeter' means.

Tell your group why you think this shape I've drawn is not a regular hexagon.

Groups of three

Give each group a set of statement cards cut from RS29. Children take turns to pick a card and read out the statement. As a group, they sort the statements into three sets: 'Possible', 'Impossible' and 'Not sure'.

Children can use rulers to check the statements.

Children then create some statements of their own to add to any of the sets.

Explain why you are not sure about that statement.

Are you confident that this one is impossible?

Support: Children work in mixed-ability groups, sharing the responsibility for ensuring that everyone understands why a statement has been sorted in a particular set.

Extend: Ask for further statements about other shapes, including facts about their diagonals and radii.

Plenary

Difficult ideas
Where some of the statements are difficult, rely on children to thrash out the ideas between themselves.

With the class, discuss the 'Not sure' set and resolve some of the issues.

Groups choose one of their own new statements and invite a member of their group to read this out. The other groups discuss briefly whether or not the statement is possible. Ask for a show of hands and sort the new statement cards into the sets, discussing those where there is disagreement.

(m) *If you have a rectangle with a perimeter of 60 cm, what could the lengths of the sides be?*

(discussion) *Is that the only possibility? Why/Why not?*

Assessment for learning

Can the children

(m) Calculate the perimeter of a regular hexagon with sides of 10 cm or 10.1 cm?

(discussion) Share in the discussion of a statement someone else has read?

(speaking) Speak confidently when telling you about a statement they are sure is impossible?

If not

(m) Demonstrate perimeters with lengths of string if the child is confused about the concept of perimeter.

(discussion) Ask the child who reads the statement to be 'Chairperson' and help the other two members of the group decide about the validity of the statement.

(smiley) Check that the work is at an appropriate level. Observe the child working with a small group of their friends and see if they are able to speak more confidently about mathematical ideas in that context.

Marking weights on a scale
Classroom technique: Peer tutoring

Introduction

Display RS30 and briefly revise with the class how to read scales. Announce a weight, move a pointer slowly from 0 kg towards 4 kg and ask the children to indicate when you reach the correct marker.

(m) *How many divisions are there between 0 and 1? So what weight does that first marker show?*

Can you explain to your group how you know that this marker is 100 g?

Groups of three

Children work in groups of three. Give each group two copies of RS30 and one copy of RS31.

Child A slowly reads out the first list of measures from RS31. Children B and C colour in those markers on their copies of the weight scale on RS30.

Child A then acts as 'Teacher', helping Child B and Child C compare their answers and sorting out any discrepancies.

Child B and Child C then each take a turn as 'Teacher'.

(m) *What do these unnumbered markers mean?*

How do you know that this marker shows 600 grams?

Kelly and Emma have got different answers. How can we help?

Speaking skills
You may want to model for children how to read out the list slowly and clearly, repeating each measure just once.

Peer tutoring
Child A is being asked to take on responsibilities that they may not be used to. Encourage children to 'have a go' – they may surprise themselves at how they rise to the challenge.

Rotating roles
This technique (p10) ensures equal participation from each member of the group. Each child will have one turn as 'Teacher' and two turns as 'Pupil'.

Support: Count with children in hundreds as they point to the markers on RS30 with a pencil. They then write in key markers such as 500 g and 1 kg 500 g.

Extend: Children rewrite the lists of measures, using decimals instead of grams and half-kilograms.

Plenary

Present various objects to the class: a shoe, an orange, a bottle of water, and so on. Each time, children estimate the weight of each object, giving reasons for the estimates: "I think the shoe weighs about 1 kilogram, because it is probably about the same as the bag of sugar."

Children check the weight on a set of scales.

Describe where the pointer is on the scale.

How many of these oranges do you think will weigh a kilogram?

Turn to a neighbour
Children turn to a neighbour who may not necessarily be someone they worked with earlier. They tell them how much they think that object might weigh and then point to that marker on their copy of RS30.

Assessment for learning

Can the children

(m) Find the markers that represent the various weights up to 5 kg?

Use appropriate language to say how they work out which marker on the scale represents which weight?

Help another child understand where they have gone wrong?

If not

(m) Help children work out the size of each interval, then practise counting in jumps of 100 g with the children, pointing to each marker as you do so.

List the vocabulary you want children to use and work with them to think up sentences using these words.

Practise similar work on scales, emphasising explanations of the reasoning.

Name _____

Self and peer assessment

Lesson 21: Measuring shapes	I think	My partner thinks
(m) I can measure lines to the nearest half-centimetre.		
I can use the words 'radius', 'diameter', 'approximately' when talking about my work.		
I can say one thing that I did well in the lesson and one thing that I need to improve.		

Lesson 22: Designing a ruler	I think	My partner thinks
(m) I make sure that the markers are at intervals of 1 centimetre on the ruler I make.		
I often choose to say something when we have a class discussion.		
I think about the needs of the user when I make a ruler.		

Self and peer assessment

Lesson 23: Perimeters of shapes	I think	My partner thinks
(m) I can work out the perimeter of a regular hexagon that has sides of 10 cm.		
(⊗) I take my turn to say something when we are discussing work in a group.		
(☺) I can say whether or not a statement is possible.		

Lesson 24: Marking weights on a scale	I think	My partner thinks
(m) I can find the places on the scale that represent 1 kilogram, 600 grams and 3!s kilograms.		
(⊗) I have used these words today: 'scale', 'marker', 'interval', 'kilogram' and 'gram'.		
(☺) I try to help someone understand where they have gone wrong.		

Shape and space

Learning objectives

	Lessons			
	25	**26**	**27**	**28**
ⓜ Maths objectives				
describe and visualise 2D shapes	●			
generalise about 2D shapes		●		
describe and name 2D shapes			●	
use all eight compass directions				●
Ⓢ Speaking and listening skills				
listen with sustained concentration	●			
contribute to small-group discussion		●	●	
listen and follow instructions accurately				●
Ⓟ Personal skills				
work with others: show awareness and understanding of others' needs	●			
organise work: plan and manage a group task		●		
improve learning and performance: assess learning progress			●	
work with others: work cooperatively with others				●

About these lessons

Lesson 25: Describing shapes

Describe and visualise 2D shapes

In this activity, children describe a shape so that their partner who cannot see it can find one the same. In the process, children describe and name 2D shapes, using the descriptions to visualise the shape required.

Listen with sustained concentration

Classroom technique: Barrier game

As children cannot see each other's shapes, they must communicate by speech, listening carefully and with concentration to what is said.

Work with others: show awareness and understanding of others' needs

Children have to think about what their partners need to know to ensure that their partners select and arrange the shapes correctly.

Lesson 26: Properties of shapes

Generalise about 2D shapes

Children use phrases written on cards to create statements about 2D shapes and then discuss whether or not they are true. In doing so, they explore some of the essential properties of these shapes.

Contribute to small-group discussion

Classroom technique: Rotating roles

Children in the group have different roles, which rotate over time. The roles require children to share and discuss their ideas, thus supporting each other's learning.

Organise work: plan and manage a group task

The group have joint responsibility for a task set by the teacher. Aiming for a clear goal supports them as they share the management of the task.

Lesson 27: Classifying shapes

Describe and name 2D shapes

Children play a game of 'Four in a line', involving matching shapes to a wide range of descriptions. They must think carefully about which of these choices fits their shape (their board has sixteen possible choices) and also suits their need to place four counters in a line.

Contribute to small-group discussion

Classroom technique: Rotating roles

Children take turns to pick a shape and read out a description that fits that shape. If there are any disagreements or uncertainties, children discuss them until they reach agreement.

Improve learning and performance: assess learning progress

Children are asked to note any words or phrases about which they are uncertain, as well as to identify any they have learned about in the course of the lesson.

Lesson 28: Compass directions

Use all eight compass directions

Children tell each other how to move a counter around a drawn safari park grid, using instructions based on the eight points of the compass.

Listen and follow instructions accurately

Classroom technique: One between two

One child tells the other which moves to make with the counter before swapping roles. Children must listen carefully to the instructions they are given and take care to give accurate instructions in turn.

Work with others: work cooperatively with others

Sharing a task means that children must cooperate in order to achieve their aim.

Describing shapes
Classroom technique: Barrier game

Learning objectives

(m) Maths
Describe and visualise 2D shapes

Speaking and listening
'Listen well'
Listen with sustained concentration

Personal skills
'Think about what other people need'
Work with others: show awareness and understanding of others' needs

(W) Words and phrases
line, corner, vertex, vertices, triangle, right-angled, top, bottom, left, right, parallel

(r) Resources
selection of flat plastic shapes for each pair:
sheets of A4 paper in two different colours
rulers and scissors

Barrier
Stand with your back to the class, or erect a screen between you and the volunteer, or have the class sit round the volunteer on the floor, while you stand a couple of metres away.

Describing shapes
Use a version of 'Devil's advocate' (p11): deliberately misunderstand the child's instructions, thus forcing them to be more precise about their descriptions.

Vocabulary
Take the opportunity to introduce vocabulary you want children to use. Define it if necessary and write it up.

Crossing lines
Make sure that the lines cross.

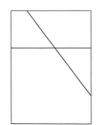

Introduction

You will need two identical sets of four shapes. Invite a volunteer to come to the front of the class to help you demonstrate the activity. Give the volunteer one set of shapes and ask them to arrange them in a line in any order – in view of the class, but hidden from you.

The volunteer describes the shapes and their order so that you can arrange yours in the same way (on an overhead projector if possible, so that the children can see). As you go along, ask questions as necessary to clarify what is meant.

(m) *I've got two shapes like that. I need more information.*

(m) *Which way up?*

(m) *You said, "Place the shape with its sharpest angle pointing upwards." What do you mean?*

Pairs

Give each pair of children two sheets of paper in two different colours. Ask them to draw two intersecting straight lines at any angle right across one sheet of paper, then to put the sheets of paper together and cut along the drawn lines, making two identical sets of polygonal shapes in different colours.

Children sit back to back with their partner. Child A arranges their shapes in an arbitrary order and describes this to Child B. Child B replicates the arrangement with their shapes.

Pairs then swap roles and repeat the activity.

(m) *You told Ed to take the biggest shape. Do you mean the longest shape or the one with the biggest area?*

(s) *You said to put it next to the first shape, but you didn't say which side.*

(p) *I wonder if you are giving your partner enough information about that shape.*

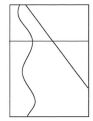

Support: Choose just two of the pieces to work with.

Extend: Children draw three or four lines. They could include one curved line.

Plenary

Display a set of four shapes and have a class brainstorm of all the words and phrases that could be used to describe them. Scribe these.

> 4 sides
> 4 angles
> 4 vertices
> two right angles
> one angle more than a right angle
> one angle less than a right angle
> all sides different lengths
> 2 parallel sides

Take each shape in turn and ask for suggestions about how to describe the orientation of the shape.

(m) *What can you say about the sides of this shape?*

(m) *Can you convince me that this angle is more than a right angle?*

(m) *Put the longest side of the triangle parallel to the bottom of the board.*

Assessment for learning

Can the children

(m) Use a range of vocabulary to describe their shapes?

(S) Repeat the description given by their partner and identify a shape that matches?

(☺) Speak clearly and readily repeat what they said if asked to do so?

If not

(m) Note any words that are not being used widely and do some focused teaching.

(S) Ask children to repeat back a description broken into smaller chunks: "It's got four sides"; "It's got one right angle", and so on. Do more activities that involve listening skills, in other subjects as well as in mathematics.

(☺) Have a discussion with the class about what it feels like to need help from a partner and how children want their partner to behave.

Properties of shapes
Classroom technique: Rotating roles

Learning objectives

m **Maths**
Generalise about 2D shapes

Speaking and listening
'Join in a discussion with a small group'
Contribute to small-group discussion

Personal skills
'Manage a group task'
Organise work: manage a group task

W **Words and phrases**
symmetrical, regular, irregular, pentagon, hexagon, heptagon, octagon, polygon, quadrilateral, convex, concave

r **Resources**
for each pair:
strips cut from RS32 and RS33
shapes reference sheet
selection of flat plastic shapes
rulers
wipe boards

U&A Counter-examples
Children use their wipe boards to draw shapes to disprove statements.

"Circles aren't concave. Concave shapes go inwards like this."

True or false?
Make sure that the discussion winds up with a statement of the true state of affairs. It is important that children are allowed to think and argue about shapes, but also that they are clear in the end about what is true and what is not.

Rotating roles
'Turns' pass to the left. The child to the right of the one who has just had their turn takes on the role of 'Chairperson', making sure that everyone has their say and gets heard.

U&A General statements
Making general statements and testing their truth is an important mathematical activity, which can give children an overview of the relationships between different kinds of shapes.

Introduction

Children work in pairs. Give each pair a selection of flat shapes and a shapes reference sheet.

Divide the strips cut from RS32 and RS33 into two piles, according to whether they are white or shaded, and lay the two piles face down on the desk in front of you. On the board, write up three headings: 'Always', 'Sometimes' and 'Never'. Choose one strip at random from each pile, read out the words on the two cards as one statement and write the statement on the board.

octagons	have more than two sides

Pairs discuss whether or not the statement is true, referring to their own shapes or the reference sheet.

Ask for comments on your statement. If someone disagrees, invite that child to argue against the statement and encourage a general discussion.

Rewrite the statement under the appropriate heading on the board.

m *Ruby says, "This semicircle is regular." Is this statement true?*

m *Is it always true that pentagons have no right angles? Try to draw one that does.*

Groups of four

Pairs join in groups of four. Children repeat the same activity as in the introduction, taking turns to take *at random* two strips to make a statement and discussing under which heading ('Always', 'Sometimes' or 'Never') the statement would belong.

Identify any ideas that you want children to share in the plenary and tell the children which statement you want them to talk about.

m *What is a 'regular' shape?*

⊙ *See what the others in your group think about your idea.*

☺ *Is everyone getting a chance to say what they think?*

Support: Children work in mixed-ability groups.

Extend: Give children mathematical dictionaries and ask them to add their own shapes and descriptions to the sets of cards – for example, 'dodecagon'; 'has two pairs of parallel sides'.

Plenary

1, 2, 3, 4
If you use this technique (p12) to decide which member of the group speaks, remind children earlier in the lesson that you will call on them later. Alternatively, ask groups to appoint their own speaker.

Groups choose one of their statements to share with the class, stating under which heading they wrote it, and why.

Take the opportunity to underline any teaching points and clarify any confusion.

(m) *You can have a concave quadrilateral. Can you have a concave triangle?*

(m) *Draw me an example of a polygon with fewer than three sides.*

(s) *Discuss with your group whether that is a 'Sometimes' statement or a 'Never' statement.*

Assessment for learning

Can the children

(m) Recognise the truth (or otherwise) of at least some of the statements they create?

(s) Allow other children in the group a chance to speak and listen to them without interrupting?

(☺) Work together to decide whether ten or more statements are 'always', 'sometimes' or 'never' true?

If not

(m) Do some work making shapes from geostrips or straws and sorting them, using the criteria on RS33.

(s) Use a 'talking stick' (p10) both in small-group work and in whole-class discussion.

(☺) Observe this group working again and note the dynamics that prevent them achieving their task. Then rearrange the grouping so that children who work effectively can model good practice to others.

Classifying shapes
Classroom technique: Rotating roles

Possible sorting set descriptors
– more than 4 sides
– not square
– all sides straight
– fewer than 5 vertices
– triangle or square
– convex
– not a regular polygon
– one line of symmetry

Reaching agreement
Everyone must agree. If they don't, children should talk about it until they do reach agreement.

Introduction

Shuffle the shape cards cut out from RS34 and put them in a pile, face down. Turn over the top card and show it to the children. Ask for words that describe it.

Take another card and repeat the process. Then display a set of six shapes and ask for words that describe the set.

How can we check whether this shape has sides that are all the same length?

Tell your neighbour how you know for sure that this shape is not a regular polygon.

Pairs/Groups of four

Children work in pairs, sorting out the shapes. Give each pair a collection of shapes cut from RS34. Each pair puts together a set of shapes that has a common property or can be described in the same words. When the pair is satisfied with their set, they write down the description of the shapes.

Pairs then join with another pair and take it in turns to display their set and ask the other pair to work out what they have written on their paper. When both pairs have successfully worked out the property of each other's set, the children swap pieces of paper and re-sort their shapes so that the properties of their new shape set matches the paper they were given.

(m) *Are only squares described as having 'four right angles'?*

How can you prove to your group that this shape has a line of symmetry?

Which descriptions were you not sure about?

Support: Children sort the shapes into a set.

Extend: Children sort all the shapes into sets and give each set a label.

Plenary

A pair of children displays one of their sets, and the rest of the class suggest other shapes that could be part of that set. The pair must say whether or not the new shape can be in the set, giving reasons for acceptance or refusal.

(m) *Can you explain whether or not a triangle can go in this set of right-angled shapes?*

Assessment for learning

Can the children

(m) Find at least one description to correspond with any 2D shape you offer them?

(discussion icon) Stay silent while another child is speaking?

(face icon) Identify one or more words or phrases that they have come to understand better during the course of the lesson?

If not

(m) Suggest that children work in pairs so that a child having problems is supported by a confident partner.

(discussion icon) Remind children that good manners are important. If necessary, use the 'Talking stick' technique (p10).

(face icon) Encourage children's ability to self-assess by starting a lesson with a test on simple shape facts that they mark themselves.

Compass directions
Classroom technique: One between two

Tell your partner
Tell children to discuss with their partner what they think your best move is each time. Ask for suggestions and take a show of hands to find the most popular each time.

Number of trips
There are four pairs of animals – enough for four trips of this kind. However, children can also make trips between different animals, as you did in the introduction.

One between two
Child A makes the decisions; Child B asks for clarification or suggests alternative moves.

Introduction

Display RS35 and model the activity that you want the children to do. You are visiting a safari park. Choose an animal to start your trip from and place a counter on that square of the grid. Choose a different animal to finish your tour of the park and circle it.

The aim is to move from one animal to the other with as few moves as possible.

Children work out one move at a time for you to make, according to the rules given at the bottom of the sheet.

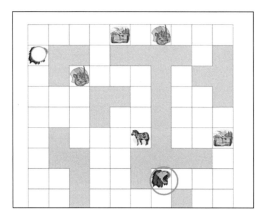

Move 2 squares south

Keep a tally of the moves you make.

(m) *How do I work out where south-east is?*

(m) *Is there a quicker way for me to move from here to there?*

Pairs

Pairs of children do the same activity, but aim to get from one animal to the other matching one.

Child A instructs Child B which moves to make and keeps a tally of the moves.

Partners then swap roles for the next trip.

(m) *What kind of directions allow you to move diagonally?*

(s) *Tell me what Zahir just said to you.*

(p) *How can you make it easier for your partner to understand what you mean?*

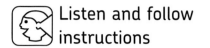
Support: Restrict moves through the safari park to North, South, East or West.

Extend: Children try to beat their own score for any particular trip. Remove the letters 'W', 'S' and 'E' from the compass symbol above the park, so that children have to work these out for themselves. Children also devise a similar route for another pair to work on.

Plenary

Pairs place their copy of RS35 in front of them, with their counters on a particular square (for example, the square in the extreme north-west). Instruct everybody to make a move, then make the same move with your own counter on your grid.

Pairs discuss which move would take them back to where they were.

(m) *Will moving five squares south-east get me back to where I was?*

(m) *Tell me which move to do to get to the lion on the line above where I am now.*

Assessment for learning

Can the children

(m) Say the direction in which you have moved your counter, using all eight compass directions?

(S) Move their counter as instructed by their partner?

(☺) Complete several trips successfully, working with their partner?

If not

(m) Check that children can use the main four directions successfully. Consider using 'Peer tutoring' (p8) to explain how the eight compass directions work.

(S) Suggest that children repeat their partner's instruction back to the partner as a check before moving the counter.

(☺) Talk with the children about what 'working cooperatively' means and write up some cooperative working aims to refer to in future lessons. Make sure you praise children who work well together and achieve the task they were set.

Name

Self and peer assessment

Lesson 25: Describing shapes	I think	My partner thinks
(m) I can describe shapes and how to arrange them.		
(🗩) I can repeat back the description my partner has just given.		
(😊) I try to speak clearly so my partner can hear me properly.		

Lesson 26: Properties of shapes	I think	My partner thinks
(m) I can usually tell whether the statement I have made is true.		
(🗩) I give other children a chance to speak.		
(😊) I listen to people without interrupting.		

Name

Lesson 27: Classifying shapes	I think	My partner thinks
(m) I can say something mathematical about any 2D shape.		
I keep quiet when another child is speaking.		
I understand some words better now because of this lesson.		

Lesson 28: Compass directions	I think	My partner thinks
(m) I can use all eight compass directions.		
I can move the counter as my partner tells me to.		
I have worked well with my partner.		

Self and peer assessment

Resource sheets

Name _____   RS1

✂

Thousands	Hundreds	Tens	Ones		Thousands	Hundreds	Tens	Ones

Maths Out Loud Year 4   Lesson 1

Name _____   RS2

Critical evaluation

• What did you learn in this activity?

• How many marks out of 10 would you give yourself for listening today?

• If you found something difficult, what did you do?

• What did you do about any mistakes you made?

Maths Out Loud Year 4   Lesson 1

Name _____   RS3

✂

Is it greater than 5000?
Is it between ☐ and ☐ ?
Is it greater than ☐ ?
Is the digit in the thousands place a ☐ ?
Is it less than 4999?
Is the tens digit even?
Is it less than ☐ ?
Are all its digits different?

Maths Out Loud Year 4   Lesson 2

Name _____   RS4

✂

Is it greater than 500?
Is it between ☐ and ☐ ?
Is it greater than ☐ ?
Is the digit in the tens place a ☐ ?
Is it less than 299?
Is the hundreds digit even?
Is it less than ☐ ?
Are all its digits different?

Maths Out Loud Year 4   Lesson 2

RS5

Name _____ RS5

Make a string of 8 tree lights.
Use three colours.
½ the lights must be the same colour.

| | of the lights are _____
| | of the lights are _____
| | of the lights are _____

Make a string of 10 tree lights.
Use three colours.
½ the lights must be the same colour.

| | of the lights are _____
| | of the lights are _____
| | of the lights are _____

Make a string of 12 tree lights.
Use three colours.
½ the lights must be the same colour.

| | of the lights are _____
| | of the lights are _____
| | of the lights are _____

Maths Out Loud Year 4   Lesson 5

RS6

Name _____ RS6

Make a string of 8 tree lights.
Use two colours.
½ the lights must be the same colour.

| | of the lights are _____
| | of the lights are _____

Make a string of 10 tree lights.
Use two colours.
½ the lights must be the same colour.

| | of the lights are _____
| | of the lights are _____

Make a string of 12 tree lights.
Use two colours.
½ the lights must be the same colour.

| | of the lights are _____
| | of the lights are _____

Maths Out Loud Year 4   Lesson 5

RS7

Name _____ RS7

Make a string of 12 tree lights.
Use three colours.
½ the lights must be red, ¼ must be green.

| | of the lights are _____
| | of the lights are _____
| | of the lights are _____
| | of the lights are _____

Make a string of 14 tree lights.
Use three colours.
½ the lights must be blue, 1/7 must be red.

| | of the lights are _____
| | of the lights are _____
| | of the lights are _____
| | of the lights are _____

Make a string of 16 tree lights.
Use three colours.
½ the lights must be red, ¼ must be yellow.

| | of the lights are _____
| | of the lights are _____
| | of the lights are _____
| | of the lights are _____

Maths Out Loud Year 4   Lesson 5

RS8

Name _____ RS8

Maths Out Loud Year 4   Lesson 6

Name _____ RS9

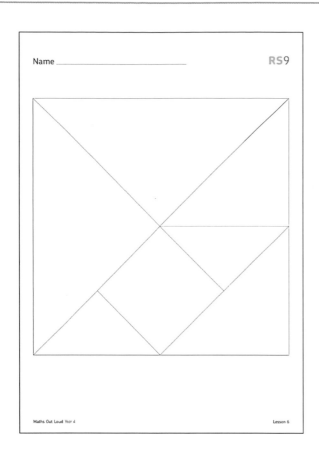

Name _____ RS10

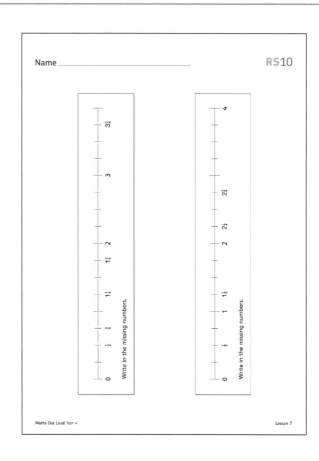

Write in the missing numbers.

Name _____ RS11

Number	Change to	How?	Check
2.7	2	−0.7	✔
2.7	0.7		
5.5	0.5		
7.1	7		
45.6	45		
21	20		
2.1	0.1		
36.7	30.7		
456.9	406.9		
45.6	45		

Name _____ RS12

Tens	Ones	tenths
	0.	

RS13

Name _____

☐ ☐ + ☐ = 100

☐ ☐ + ☐ = 100

☐ ☐ + ☐ = 100

☐ ☐ + ☐ = 100

RS14

Name _____

☐ ☐ ☐ + ☐ = 500

☐ ☐ ☐ + ☐ = 500

RS15

Name _____

8	22	15	10	26
23	14	9	24	11
16	3	27	12	17
21	25	13	19	4
7	20	6	5	18

RS16

Name _____

8	15	10	14	9
11	16	3	12	17
13	4	7	6	5
18	15	10	14	9
16	3	12	17	11

RS17

Name _____ RS17

Cafe in the Park

soup and roll	£1.10
pizza slice	£1.25
filled roll	£1.30
bag of crisps	45p
apple	35p
banana	38p
orange	40p
chocolate bar	99p
milk	45p
fruit juice	60p
cola	80p

RS18

Name _____ RS18

Which table?

6	16	12	20
4	28	8	40
50	30	40	20
24	12	32	8
8	6	20	2
35	50	20	10
40	16	28	36
12	18	6	30

2×
3×
4×
5×
6×
10×

Find the odd one out

60	27	90	40
50	15	21	35
23	12	36	40
18	7	20	8
30	21	32	12
32	16	9	40
12	8	9	21
8	6	12	29

2×
3×
4×
5×
10×

RS19

Name _____ RS19

1	2	3	4	5	6	7	8	9	10
2	4	6	8	10	12	14	16	18	20
3	6	9	12	15	18	21	24	27	30
4	8	12	16	20	24	28	32	36	40
5	10	15	20	25	30	35	40	45	50
6	12	18	24	30	36	42	48	54	60
7	14	21	28	35	42	49	56	63	70
8	16	24	32	40	48	56	64	72	80
9	18	27	36	45	54	63	72	81	90
10	20	30	40	50	60	70	80	90	100

RS20

Name _____ RS20

I am thinking of two numbers. H / M / E
I add them and get ____
I multiply them and get ____
What are they? ____ ____

I am thinking of two numbers. H / M / E
I add them and get ____
I multiply them and get ____
What are they? ____ ____

I am thinking of two numbers. H / M / E
I add them and get ____
I multiply them and get ____
What are they? ____ ____

I am thinking of two numbers. H / M / E
I add them and get ____
I multiply them and get ____
What are they? ____ ____

I am thinking of two numbers. H / M / E
I add them and get ____
I multiply them and get ____
What are they? ____ ____

I am thinking of two numbers. H / M / E
I add them and get ____
I multiply them and get ____
What are they? ____ ____

Name _____ RS21

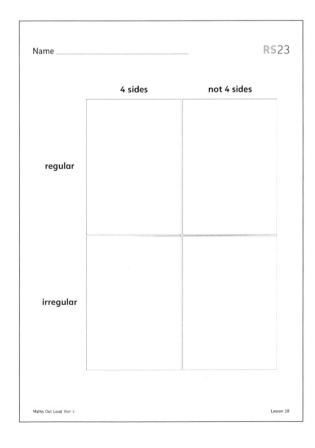

Maths Out Loud Year 4   Lesson 15

Name _____ RS22

Two-digit numbers

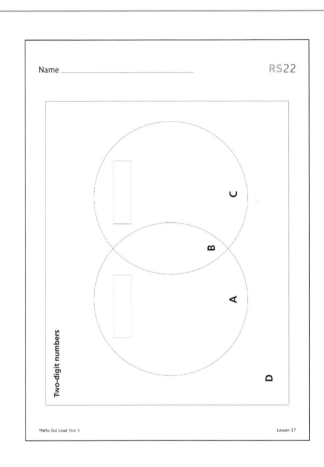

Maths Out Loud Year 4   Lesson 17

Name _____ RS23

	4 sides	not 4 sides
regular		
irregular		

Maths Out Loud Year 4   Lesson 18

Name _____ RS24

Sorcerer's Magic Shop stocktaking

dried spiders	卌 卌 卌 卌			
toad warts (packs of 5)					
worms (packs of 10)	卌 卌
1 kg jars of slime		
packs of moon dust (100 g)	卌				
packs of moon dust (500 g)	卌

Maths Out Loud Year 4   Lesson 19

124

RS25

Sorcerer's Magic Shop
Apprentice's test – true or false?

1. There are more dried spiders in stock than packs of worms. ☐ True ☐ False

2. There are ten toad warts altogether. ☐ True ☐ False

3. There is enough slime to fill two 500 ml jars. ☐ True ☐ False

4. Altogether, there is more than 1 kg of moon dust. ☐ True ☐ False

5. There are over 100 worms. ☐ True ☐ False

6. There is enough moon dust in 500 g packs to make fifteen 100 g packs. ☐ True ☐ False

7. There are not enough toad warts to make a vanishing spell (vanishing spells need 20 warts). ☐ True ☐ False

8. There are 42 dried spiders. ☐ True ☐ False

Maths Out Loud Year 4 Lesson 19

RS26

Name _____ RS26

1
2
3
4
5
6

1
2
3
4
5
6

Maths Out Loud Year 4 Lesson 20

RS27

Name _____ RS27

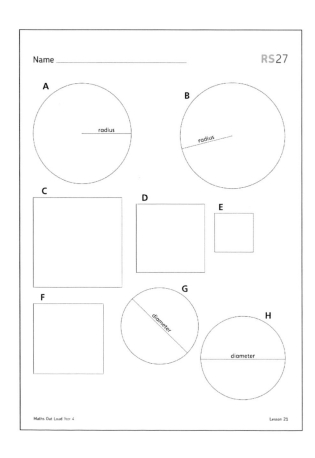

RS28

Name _____ RS28

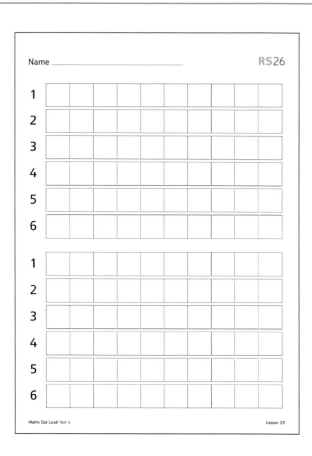
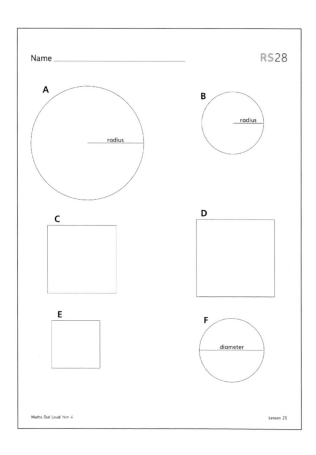

Maths Out Loud Year 4 Lesson 21

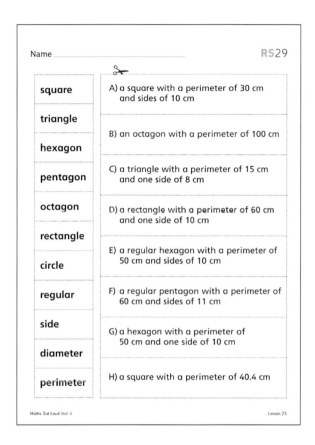

RS29

Name _____

square	A) a square with a perimeter of 30 cm and sides of 10 cm
triangle	
hexagon	B) an octagon with a perimeter of 100 cm
pentagon	C) a triangle with a perimeter of 15 cm and one side of 8 cm
octagon	D) a rectangle with a perimeter of 60 cm and one side of 10 cm
rectangle	
circle	E) a regular hexagon with a perimeter of 50 cm and sides of 10 cm
regular	F) a regular pentagon with a perimeter of 60 cm and sides of 11 cm
side	G) a hexagon with a perimeter of 50 cm and one side of 10 cm
diameter	
perimeter	H) a square with a perimeter of 40.4 cm

Maths Out Loud Year 4 · Lesson 23

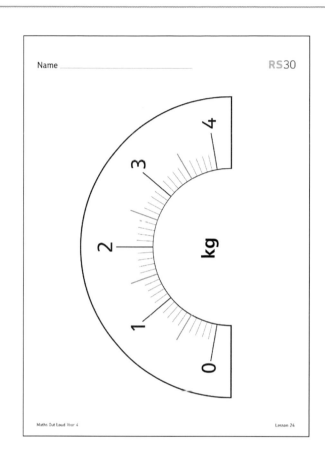

Name _____ RS30

Maths Out Loud Year 4 · Lesson 24

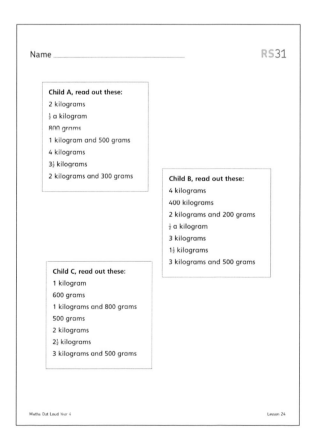

Name _____ RS31

Child A, read out these:
2 kilograms
½ a kilogram
800 grams
1 kilogram and 500 grams
4 kilograms
3½ kilograms
2 kilograms and 300 grams

Child B, read out these:
4 kilograms
400 kilograms
2 kilograms and 200 grams
½ a kilogram
3 kilograms
1½ kilograms
3 kilograms and 500 grams

Child C, read out these:
1 kilogram
600 grams
1 kilograms and 800 grams
500 grams
2 kilograms
2½ kilograms
3 kilograms and 500 grams

Maths Out Loud Year 4 · Lesson 24

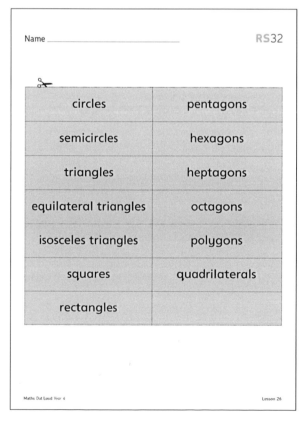

Name _____ RS32

circles	pentagons
semicircles	hexagons
triangles	heptagons
equilateral triangles	octagons
isosceles triangles	polygons
squares	quadrilaterals
rectangles	

Maths Out Loud Year 4 · Lesson 26

Name _____ RS33

have at least one right angle	are two-dimensional
are 4-sided	have more than 2 sides
have 3 or more sides	are regular
have at least one right angle	are irregular
have no right angles	have no angles equal
have fewer than 9 sides	have all sides equal
have 3 sides	are convex
are symmetrical	are concave

Maths Out Loud Year 4   Lesson 26

Name _____ RS34

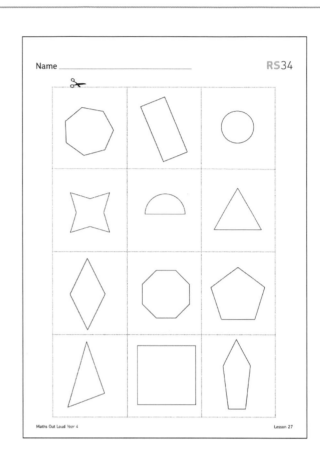

Maths Out Loud Year 4   Lesson 27

Name _____ RS35

Safari Park rules
Your aim is to move from one animal to another.
You may not move through the grey spaces.
Your journey may go through a square with an animal.
A move can go N, S, E, W, NE, NW, SE or SW.
A move can take you any number of squares in one direction.

Maths Out Loud Year 4   Lesson 28